WHAT OTHERS ARE ~~SAYING ABOUT~~

SEASON OF

"Rebecca Ingram Powell has hit the ball out of the park with this one! If you desire to truly understand, relate to, and enjoy a fantastic relationship with your middle schooler, I highly recommend that you read and re-read this power-packed, insightful book. As a result, you and your child will be deeply blessed."

Ginger Plowman,
author of *Don't Make Me Count to Three!*

"Rebecca Ingram Powell provides insight and wisdom on how to keep the *Season of Change* from becoming the storms of change. Middle school is a crucial time in your child's life. Too often it is marked by anger and frustration in both parents and children. Family relationships can easily unravel instead of becoming more closely knit. *Season of Change* gives parents a much-needed heads-up. The Toolbox section at the end of each chapter gives practical advice on how to address the most difficult problems of these years. Rebecca's counsel is both compassionate and biblical. The sections on modesty, pornography, and dating are particularly helpful."

Jay Younts,
author of *Everyday Talk*

"Rebecca Ingram Powell has a shocking message for us parents: Those middle school years aren't the years when we're waiting for the big changes to come—they *are* the years of the big changes! You put your baby to bed and then wake up to a creature who towers over you, keeps secrets, and finds you annoying. If you're feeling lost, let Rebecca's fresh and practical book be your cheering section: the motivation you need to make sure your child's season of change isn't a U-turn away from God, but instead an adventurous journey toward Him."

Sheila Wray Gregoire,
author of *To Love, Honor and Vacuum*

"This great resource from Rebecca Ingram Powell is an eye-opening look at what today's youth face when they hit the teenage years. Parents will receive encouragement and practical tips on how to direct their young adults toward making wise life decisions and to seek God with their whole hearts!"

Michelle Duggar of The Duggar Family
(featured on *The Discovery Channel***)**

Season of Change

Parenting Your Middle Schooler
with Passion and Purpose

REBECCA INGRAM POWELL

Tate Publishing *& Enterprises*

Published by Tate Publishing & Enterprises, LLC
127 E. Trade Center Terrace | Mustang, Oklahoma 73064 USA
1.888.361.9473 | www.tatepublishing.com

Tate Publishing is committed to excellence in the publishing industry. The company reflects the philosophy established by the founders, based on Psalm 68:11,
"The Lord gave the word and great was the company of those who published it."

Book design copyright © 2008 by Tate Publishing, LLC. All rights reserved.
Cover design by Kandi Evans
Interior design by Lynly D. Taylor

Published in the United States of America

ISBN: 978-1-60604-290-8

1. Christian Living: Relationships   2. Family & Relationships: Parenting
08.05.14

This book is dedicated to the ones who carried me
through my season of change:
My parents, Ted and Mary Lou Ingram,
Angie Dudley Manuel,
and most of all,
the unchanging Lord Jesus Christ.
Through life's every season, He is faithful.

ACKNOWLEDGMENTS

I am so thankful for:

My husband, Rich, who stayed after me to get this book written! You tend to my procrastinating spirit with gentle mercy, but you know how to motivate me to get up and get to it! I love you.

My three wonderful children, Danya, David, and Derek. You are such blessings! Thank you for allowing me to share your stories in these pages. Thank you for praying with me and for me. Being your mom is the greatest earthly joy of my life (even better than writing books!), and I love you all so much.

My parents-in-law, Ray and Patricia Powell, for their unwavering support and prayers.

Ginger Plowman, my dear friend. Thank you for your generosity, your encouragement, and your constant prodding! You and Rich teamed up on me to get this done, and I'm so glad you did!

William Summey, Jodi Skulley, and all the gang at *ParentLife* magazine. It has been a thrill to write for mothers each month. Thank you for that unbelievable privilege!

All the parenting experts who have shared their wisdom with me over the years of writing the "Mom's Life" column. I have learned so much from you. Thank you for your Kingdom work!

Pastor Barry Davis, Kelly Hall, Ginger Plowman, Rich Powell, and Terry Sereff. Your thoughts and comments in reading through the manuscript were so appreciated and helped make for a much better final copy!

Jesus, the Author and Finisher of our faith. Lord, when I was in middle school, You knew that one day *Season of Change* would be written. Out of the pain, You had a plan. May this book be used by You to help parents of middlers everywhere.

TABLE OF CONTENTS

INTRODUCTION

My thirteen-year-old daughter, Danya, was scrambling around her messy room, trying to pack for youth camp. I went in to see if I could help her get ready, but I stumbled over my offer when I saw "Mimi" wadded up on her bed, obviously not to be included in the packing.

"Mimi" was Danya's baby blanket. While she continued gathering her things, I went unnoticed to her bed, picked up Mimi, fluffed it out, and remembered its beginnings.

I was a new mom with a fussy baby, who, the pediatrician assured me, did not have colic. Night after night I had rocked, paced, and prayed for my crying little one to go to sleep. Night after night we stayed up. Getting her to sleep didn't seem to be the problem—it was keeping her asleep! Every time I tried to put her down, she would wake up and begin crying again.

Then one night, despite my sleepless stupor, I realized that Danya was holding on to my pink, satiny nursing gown. Whenever I put her down, she lost her grip and woke up. So that night, as I put her in her crib, I didn't peel her fingers from my gown. Instead, I peeled the gown off and laid it in the crib with her. Ah, success! A victory born of desperation but a victory nonetheless!

Now, sitting on Danya's bed holding Mimi and my memories, I realized for the first time that when I scampered off for a clean gown and the comfort of sleep that night, I had just put some distance between my baby and me. It was necessary, to be sure. But it was a huge step of separation, independence, and helping my baby grow up. Now here we were, thirteen years later, and Danya was going to camp—leaving Mimi behind. Unashamed, Mimi had gone everywhere else with this kid: her grandparents' house, family vacations, even sleepovers and slumber parties. But Mimi wasn't going to youth camp. This time, Danya was taking her own step of separation, independence, and growing up.

"So," I began, stroking Mimi and cradling it in my arms, "I guess this means you don't get to go to youth camp, Mimi."

"*Mohhhhm!*"

Yes, ladies and gentlemen, we have a seventh-grader. Now what?

The greatest challenge of these middle years is that of helping our children make their faith their own—not something we have peeled off and given them as security. Not a piece of ourselves. Certainly, our children are mosaics of us. They contain fragments of our own convictions and insecurities. They are endowed with many of our own strengths and weaknesses. Forever, they will be linked to the parents who raised them.

When it comes to faith, however, a piece of ours must

only serve as an influence, an inspiration, and an impression—not an inheritance. A personal relationship with Christ cannot be earned or inherited. A child's faith is independent of his parent's. It must be separate and distinct. While our children depend on us to introduce them to Christ, to make His Lordship known in our lives, and to make His presence known in our homes, we must depend on His Holy Spirit to do the work of transforming their lives individually.

Parenting itself oversees a series of transformations. I used to parent newborns. Within the blink of an eye, I was taking care of toddlers. Then I had preschoolers, and on it went, as my kids grew at breakneck speed. Even today, as quickly as I get accustomed to one phase of growth, those children disappear, only to be replaced by taller, prettier, stronger versions. Smarter, too.

Each new stage calls for evaluation, goal-setting, and prayer—lots of prayer! As the middle years approach, motherhood is all the more challenging. Adulthood is within view, inching closer with every moment that passes, and so, I have to ask myself some questions: What is each child holding on to? Have I planted enough seeds of Jesus to keep her hand tightly gripping His? Or will she lose her grip on Him once I let go of her?

Because eventually, inevitably, I will have to let go.

ONE

REMEMBERING MIDDLE SCHOOL

"I just don't understand her lately."
"He's like a different person."
"He doesn't talk to me anymore."
"She's changed."

hen I talk to parents of middle schoolers, they are often baffled by their children's behavior. It leads me to wonder if they have suppressed their own painful memories of those years to the point of denial. After all, they obviously survived the trauma of being thirteen! With a baffled expression of my own, I ask them, "Don't you remember middle school?"

I remember my first day. My family had just moved from Nashville, Tennessee, across the state to Knoxville, where my minister dad had taken on a new pastorate. Orientation was held in the school's large auditorium, and I was just one of a few hundred kids. Unwilling to be left alone to face the masses, I begged my mother to go in and sit with me. There were no other parents in the auditorium, and she hesitated.

"Are you sure?" she asked.

I nodded emphatically. Believe me, I was sure. I couldn't face it alone. There had already been too many changes in my life, and I was unnerved at the thought of going in front of that audience by myself. Do you remember those days of utter self-consciousness, of feeling always on display and uncomfortable?

Settling into our seats, I was very quiet, holding my breath. There was a lot of movement, noise, and laughter among the kids. I learned later that my new school was the landing place for three elementary schools, so while no one knew everyone, everyone knew someone. Everyone except me.

I heard the whispers and saw the laughing eyes when my mother sat down with me. She didn't miss it, either. A high school teacher by trade, she was always pretty up on kids. She wanted me to be able to sit there by myself, but she didn't insist, and I'm grateful for that. I didn't care what the other kids thought at that time. My fear overruled any other emotion, as fear tends to do.

As the orientation got underway and the other students were distracted, my mom slipped out and left me there—alone and scared. I remember looking around that huge auditorium and believing there was not anyone who felt as out of place as I did. Do you remember ever thinking the same thing? Believing you were the only one who didn't have the right clothes or the right hair? And not knowing what to do with the tug-of-war going on inside?

Scripture clearly disputes those feelings of being the only one with these words:

> No test or temptation that comes your way is beyond the course of what others have had to face. All you need to remember is that God will never let you down; He'll never let you be pushed past your limit; He'll always be there to help you come through it.
>
> 1 Corinthians 10:13, Msg

While everyone else seemed happy, secure, and surrounded by friends, according to God's Word, every single person in that room would experience loneliness at some point in their lives, and many already had. Many, like me, were scared stiff at that very moment in time. What's more, although I felt alone, I wasn't. God was there, too.

Soon we were assigned homeroom teachers and dismissed. As I left the auditorium and became part of the throng of students heading to class, a girl whom I will never forget, Teresa, walked alongside me and asked, "What's your name?" Those three simple words said welcome, friendship, and hope to one very lonely girl.

Yes, I remember middle school. In fact, I'll never forget the crash course spelled out for me on that first day.

Parents were on the outside.

Friends were all-important.

Teachers were suspect.

And suddenly, popularity was a crucial element of daily life. It was a game to be played and to be won, for some, at any cost. The paradigm had shifted; life had changed, and it wasn't just because I had moved. No, the summer between fifth and sixth grade held changes for almost everybody. It was time to fall into step or be dragged underneath the feet of the crowd. Standing out—or standing up—was clearly not an option.

Couple Madness

In Nashville, the fifth-grade class at my small Christian school was just on the verge of *the change*, that magical time when hormones explode and boys and girls begin to *like* each other. Paul and Missy were the first "couple" in my elementary school experience, and Brian and Rhonda soon followed. It was interesting. It began happening toward the end of the school year, in the spring. While I had started noticing boys by then, having two couples morph out of goofy ten- and eleven-year-old kids was still sort of mind-boggling.

By the time I arrived in middle school, it was full blown. Couple madness. Over the summer, everyone had decided middle school meant it was time to grow up and pair up. And now, there was even a social ladder, its mysterious rungs silently dictating how high you could climb.

In elementary school, there was an "everybody is friends" mentality, but on Planet Middle School, the social lines were quickly drawn—and as immovable as a federal property line. Brandon James, a minister to middle schoolers, says children will inevitably struggle with their identity because of all the changes they are experiencing and all the changes the kids around them are facing at the same time. "It is at this stage they begin asking the question, *Who am I?*" he explains. "They want to fit in and be normal no matter what it takes. In the past, they were friends with whomever they were around. Now they choose friends based on their likes and dislikes."[1]

At my new school, there was one girl in particular who ran a tight clique that called all the shots. I spent a great deal of time studying Lindy[2] and trying to figure out the essence of popularity. *Why was she popular? What was it that was different about her? How did she get to be the queen bee?* The puzzle, quite frankly, intrigued me. I vowed to get to the bottom of it, and that's sort of where I ended up. All my sleuthing brought me to the only thing I could figure was the difference between who was in and who was out: It had to be the shoes.

Got Shoes?

Lindy and her friends had beautiful Nike tennis shoes, the exact same color and style. I had no-name, no-brand shoes, and they mocked me for it. Those white Nikes were the only thing those girls had in common, so I assumed those shoes were the key to popularity. Since I knew that my folks were not about to buy me a new pair of expensive tennis shoes on a preacher's and a teacher's salaries, I figured my claim to fame was lost at sea. Then, at Christmastime, I spotted a pair of those Nikes, just my size, on a clearance table. What luck! I didn't realize, of course, that there was a closeout on the shoes because they were about to be last year's model. I asked for them for Christmas, got them, and wore them proudly to school after Christmas break—only to see Lindy and her friends strutting their stuff in new Nikes, now having another reason to make fun of me.

Mean girls. They have been around forever. They are as ancient as human nature and something all women have had to endure at some point in their lives. I honestly thought I had put those memories behind me, buried them with forgiveness and grace—until, right around the age of eleven, my daughter began experiencing certain trials of her own with mean girls. I relived some painful personal memories as I watched her wade into the turbulent waters of adolescence, where the mean girls, like sharks, still circle around their prey. I was all too familiar with their mode of operation because, in twenty-five years, nothing had changed. They smell the blood of insecurity and awkwardness, seeking prey that is obviously weakened from coping with a changing body and an unwelcome discomfiture. Their menu varies like a seaside restaurant offering the "catch of the day." They head toward their current target with alarming speed, intent upon sinking their teeth into the tender flesh of budding self-awareness—all for the singular purpose of feeling better about themselves.

Instinctively, I tried to head off the sharks before they could get too close to my daughter. I offered loads of advice and platitudes, poisoned (unfortunately) with bitterness for the mean girls that visited the beach of my youth. My husband stepped in with a word of caution.

"You are getting too involved in this," he warned.

I stepped back. I realized that I was obsessed with rescue. Somehow, I had gone from being a mother to being the coast guard. Like Richard Dreyfuss in *Jaws*, I was consumed with ridding my family's previously calm waters from this invasion by the mean girls, because I remembered. Do you?

Oddly enough, I approached my middle school years with probably the best set of circumstances of any of my classmates. I came from an unbroken, idyllic home. My mom and dad loved each other, and they loved my sister and me. Perhaps that's why it was so difficult to understand why I didn't get the same love and acceptance from my classmates. For the rest of my school years, I stayed pretty angry about the injustice of the whole in-crowd mentality, my frustration stemming largely from the fact that there simply wasn't anything that I could do about it.

My story is not all that different from other people's, maybe even yours. I know there are people with great memories of their wonder years and people with far worse reminiscences. If you dare to remember middle school, your stroll down memory lane may not be all sunshine and flowers. Speaking of the teen years, Paul David Tripp, in his book, *Age of Opportunity*, says:

> These years are hard for us [parents] because they rip back the curtain and expose us. This is why trials are so difficult, yet so useful in God's hands. We don't radically change in a moment of trial. No, trials expose what we have always been. Trials bare things to which we would have otherwise been blind. So, too, the teen years expose our self-righteousness, our impatience, our unforgiving spirit, our lack of servant love, the weakness of our faith, and our craving for comfort and ease.

In other words, as our kids confront the same challenges we faced, we will relive them. We will find out what we have really forgiven from those days and what we are still clinging to as adults. We will discover some things about ourselves that God is ready for us to deal with. We'll see how far we have come, but we'll get up close and personal with the truth of how far we have to go.

Recently, I was talking with a friend I had not seen in years. We went to middle school together. She still lives in the town where we grew up, and she was catching me up on several old friends. Then she mentioned that she had seen Lindy at a weight loss support group, and these days, the most popular girl was sporting a great deal of extra weight. I am ashamed to admit I could not suppress a smile at this information, and a delicious thrill of pleasure ran through my wicked flesh at the news. I had to repent before God because those feelings were wrong. I realized, in spite of all the years that had passed, I had not totally forgiven her. If I had, I would not have been rejoicing in her difficulties. Still offended by the way I perceived I had been treated, I remained stuck in the middle of sixth grade.

Lest you think I was always a victim, I have another confession to make and another mean girl to tell you about. There was a girl in my class, Michelle, who was a little awkward and tended to be shy. She tried hard, but for all her perseverance, she never fit in. She was always left out, mocked, or simply ignored. One day, Michelle called another girl in our class and asked for her help. She explained that she wanted and needed a friend. But the mean girl she called refused to be her friend. "I just don't like you, Michelle," she said. "I don't want to be your friend." Then as Michelle began to cry, this awful, mean girl hung up on her. Guess who the mean girl was? Right. I am so sorry, Michelle. I really am.

Parenting a middle schooler requires us to be real and vulnerable, remembering what those days were like and respecting the trials our kids are going through. As God reaches deeply into our hearts to expose the remaining crumbs of insecurity, unforgiveness, and envy, we will be liberated. The truth will set us free! But be warned: If those chains have become too comfortable, if we have become calloused from their chafing, wrenching them off will be painful.

————————————————————————— Toolbox

FACTORS OF FORGIVENESS

Remembering middle school may cause old hurts and painful memories to surface. Let's get those out of the way right now by remembering these factors of forgiveness.

F 'Fess up. Nobody's perfect. Everyone has sinned, and everyone needs forgiveness. Admit your sin to God. "[F]or all have sinned and fall short of the glory of God" (Romans 3:23, NIV).

O Open your heart. Are you willing to accept the reality of God's mercy and grace? No matter what you've done, forgiveness is yours for the asking, all because of Jesus. Incredible! "If we confess our sins, He is faithful and just and will forgive us our sins and purify us from all unrighteousness" (1 John 1:9, NIV).

R Release your hold on sin. Turn away from the temptation to repeat your past mistakes, whatever they are. "[I]f My people, who are called by My name, will humble themselves and pray and seek My face and turn from their wicked ways, then will I hear from heaven and will forgive their sin and will heal their land" (2 Chronicles 7:14, NIV).

G Give it away. Now that you've been forgiven, forgive others. Forgive freely, just as you have been forgiven. "Bear with each other and forgive whatever grievances you may have against one another. Forgive as the Lord forgave you" (Colossians 3:13, NIV).

I Initiate the actions of forgiveness. "But I tell you who hear Me: Love your enemies, do good to those who hate you, bless those who curse you, pray for those who mistreat you" (Luke 6:27–28, NIV).

V Verbalize the truth. When you are tempted to doubt the fact that you have been forgiven, say this verse aloud: "If you, O Lord, kept a record of sins, O Lord, who could stand? But with You there is forgiveness; therefore You are feared" (Psalm 130:3–4, NIV). When you are tempted to remember someone's sin against you, say this verse aloud: [Love] is not rude, it is not self-seeking, it is not easily angered, it keeps no record of wrongs" (1 Corinthians 13:5, NIV).

E Express your thanks. Thank God for the merciful, loving way He forgives you. Thank Him for enabling you to forgive others. "The Lord is my strength and my shield; my heart trusts in Him, and I am helped. My heart leaps for joy and I will give thanks to Him in song" (Psalm 28:7, NIV).

TWO

SOUNDS LIKE THIRTEEN TO ME

An Arkansas mom sat through one of my seminars with her eyes fixed fast and her body barely moving. No sooner had I concluded the workshop than she was at my side.

"You just described my daughter!" she exclaimed. "Ever since she entered middle school, she has been a different child!" She went on to explain that her beautiful, talented sixth-grader had become withdrawn and closed since school had begun that fall. Day after day, this spunky, outgoing girl came home from school discouraged, defeated, and depressed. So from four o'clock in the afternoon until bedtime, this mom and her husband lifted, cheered, and encouraged their daughter. The next morning, they sent her back to school where the cycle started all over again. By Christmas of that year, they chose to pull their daughter out of school. For this particular mom, the right decision for her family was choosing to homeschool through the middle school years.

The middle school years are part of the process of growing

up. No matter how a child is educated during these years—homeschool, public school, or private school—the events, the words, the sights, the sounds, the memories, the feelings, the crushes, the defeats, the sighs, and the desperate hopelessness of some days are forever written on the heart. Adolescence defines who we are as adults. It is part of the becoming, and at the same time, although it is a mere season of earthly life, it is rife with eternal significance for each of us and for the impact we have on others.

The Transition

Adolescence is the transitional stage of growing up. It is how God births an adult. If you are your child's biological mother, you remember what it was like being pregnant. I was so into it! I read everything I could get my hands on that had to do with labor and delivery. That was the final frontier of my pregnancy, and I wanted to know exactly what was going to happen, when it was going to happen, and why it was going to happen. I wanted all the details.

It was interesting to read about the transitional point of labor. I was determined to have a drug-free delivery (no epidural), and as I studied, I knew this would be the hardest part. Transition is the stage that occurs just before it is time to push. It is known for being the shortest stage of labor, but it is also the most painful. Contractions hit hard and fast at this point, coming like waves every two to three minutes and lasting a minute or longer. You shake, you shiver, and you become nauseous. You think you can't go on.

Sounds like thirteen to me! It's excruciating. You are almost there, almost an adult, but it is not time to push. You feel like you should be independent, but it is not time to go it alone. Your body is capable of reproducing, but you are nowhere near ready to be reproductive. All of these feelings make your head swim as you draw your knees to your chest and scream in frustration.

I've gone through natural childbirth three times, and I can tell you my success was due largely to the support I had in place. I had my husband by my side, and I always had a friend with me. It was the friend's job not to talk to me but to read God's Word to me, to wipe my brow, and to keep out of the doctor's way. That might be comparable to your role in the life of your budding teenager. This time, an adult is being birthed. Do you need to keep talking? Yes, if you know that what you are saying is God's truth—not your opinion, but wisdom you have gleaned from Him. It is your job to wipe your child's tears through the pain; in this way, your quiet, capable presence provides comfort and support. And part of your role is to keep out of the way when Jesus steps in to do the work He alone is qualified to do. As a parent, reaching the stage of transition means you keep the big picture in mind, but you focus on taking things one contraction at a time.

True North

Recently, a *Time* magazine article entitled "Is Middle School Bad for Kids?" by Claudia Wallis, stated that communities across the nation are questioning whether middle schools are really the best choice for "this volatile age group." The article offers data from a study by California's Rand Corporation, which included these statistics:

- More than half of eighth-graders fail to achieve expected levels of proficiency in reading, math and science on national tests.

- In international ratings of math achievement, U.S. students rank about average—ninth out of seventeen—at grade four, but sink to twelfth place by grade eight setting the stage for further slippage in high school.

- Reported levels of emotional and physical problems are higher among U.S. middle school students than among their peers in all eleven other countries surveyed by the World Health Organization. The same "health behavior" survey found that U.S. middle schoolers have the most negative views of the climate of their schools and peer culture.

- Crime takes off in middle school. Statistics from 1996–97 show that while 45% of public elementary schools reported one or more incidents to the police, the figure jumps to 74% for middle schools—almost as high as high schools (77%).[3]

It is no wonder that the Rand group tagged the middle school years the "Bermuda Triangle" of adolescence.

The Bermuda Triangle, also known as the Devil's Triangle, is a triangular-shaped region in the Atlantic Ocean, bound by the harbors of Bermuda, Puerto Rico, and Florida. Since the 1940s, media reports have claimed that ships and aircrafts have disappeared mysteriously from this vicinity, their pilots and crew members never found. Yet as far back as Christopher

Columbus, long before contemporary media, strange phenomena has been recorded in this area. In fact, in 1492, as the Nina, the Pinta, and the Santa Maria sailed through this zone, Columbus's compass went haywire. He recorded these compass malfunctions in his journal, adding that he and his crew saw weird lights in the sky and a bolt of fire that fell into the sea. He also reported seeing light on the horizon.[4]

From the account given in Columbus's own journal, historians believe that his compass's inaccuracy stemmed from nothing more than the discrepancy between true north and magnetic north. What's the difference? True north is a constant and refers to the geographic North Pole. Magnetic north tends to shift and refers to the pull of the Earth's magnetic field. Traveling through this particular part of the globe, the two collide. The seas get rough, and sailing is rocky. And so it is with the middle years. Traveling through this particular part of life, the precepts of God and the pull of the world collide. God's principles, like true north, are constant. The world's appeal—its ideas, definitions, and standards—tends to shift. Like the ships that sailed innocently into the Bermuda Triangle, our kids drift in to middle school, and they get lost. Too often, their internal compasses cannot find true north.

Refocusing

Clearly, middle school is a time when a child's values and identity are questioned. They begin to shrug off what they once held dear in an effort to conform to peer expectations. This often surfaces as a sudden disinterest in a sport or musical instrument they have studied throughout childhood. In some way, kids believe letting go of a childhood activity is akin to letting go of childhood. How does a parent know when to allow that shedding and when to step in and help a child to simply refocus his efforts? After all, for many children, music and dance lessons, along with participation in sports, have not been merely perceived as activities but as investments.

Joyce Pelletier, a Licensed Clinical Professional Counselor (LCPC) from Portland, Maine, encourages parents to take a good look at their parenting goals and the goals of their child by asking themselves these questions:

- How is this activity going to impact my child's career in the future?

- Does he really have the makings of a professional musician/athlete/performer?

- Do his teachers or coaches believe there is a gift?

- Why does he want to drop out?

- Does he love the activity but hate the instructor?

- Does he feel bullied by the team?

"If you are certain there's an important reason to continue, then make the necessary changes which will inspire the child to hang in there, by changing teams or instructors," Joyce says. "Have a good talk about the long-range benefits, and use rewards and consequences to maintain practice routines."[5] This is a season to challenge your child. Give him a glimpse of the future by showing him professionals hard at work on their craft, whether it is sports, dance, music, or art.

After a disappointing baseball season, my son David, then

ten, was thinking of giving up the sport he loved. We took a family trip to the Louisville Slugger Museum in Louisville, Kentucky, and spent an afternoon touring the bat factory and adjoining museum filled with memorabilia from Major League Baseball. Freshly inspired, David spent the off season that year training for the coming spring. He created a personal workout program and designed his own weight-training routine. After seeing what he could do and be, David recognized the losing season as a learning experience and resolved to practice more. His hard work paid off the following spring when he helped his team have a winning season and earn the championship.

When it comes to their gifts, children are not blank canvases on which we can paint the pictures we want to see. They are not empty hard drives that can be programmed to produce a desired result. They are born with certain talents, abilities, and personalities, hard-wired by their Creator. Ancient Jerusalem's King Solomon, the writer of many Old Testament proverbs, once said, "Train a child in the way he should go, and when he is old he will not turn from it" (Proverbs 22:6, NIV). His words indicate that part of our job as parents is to help each child realize his own unique design and train him to go with it, not against it. If we want our children to lead focused lives that make the most of their God-given talents and abilities, we must be attentive to the clues that will help us diagnose our kids' gifts and encourage their interests.

What does your child like to do? What does she like to watch others doing? My friend Marla discovered her daughter Rebecca had a talent for dancing when she was just four years old. "I think God was in it from the very beginning," she says.

She had taken Rebecca to a friend's dance studio and allowed her to participate in a class. "From the first class, I could tell she was in her element. In the weeks that followed, I actually saw her face change when she entered the studio. She became determined, purposeful, and intent on learning."

By the time she was ten, Rebecca knew that serving God through dance was what she wanted to do. Through middle school, Rebecca never wavered in her purpose. Instead, it carried her through those years, providing a focus and a framework to each day.

Contrast that with my story. During that pivotal sixth-grade year, my study of piano was detoured by my family's move. We had to find a new teacher, and it was not easy. I had been studying under the same instructor since I was five years old. She had me enrolled in music competitions and participating in seasonal recitals. Piano kept me quite busy and could have been a good outlet for me through the middle years. Instead, the challenges of a middle school mentality crept in. My mother found a very young teacher, fresh out of college and newly married. Studying for her master's, this gal was what I can best describe as a music nerd. She was definitely passionate about all things piano, but she was just a little too "out there" to connect with a peer-oriented, cool-conscious teen. After trying two more teachers over the next few years, my mom finally relented and let me drop out of music.

Similarly, my daughter began taking piano at the age of six. By the time she was ten, she was already writing songs and composing wonderfully complex piano pieces. Along came sixth grade, and she became part of the youth worship band at church. She was also playing basketball. When her schedule got crowded, she came to me, begging to take some time off from piano. I couldn't do it. I was literally scared to death that she would abandon her music study, and I knew that she was born to worship God through song. I went straight to her teacher, who agreed to work with Danya more on her original compositions, even allowing her to perform these pieces in recitals rather than the traditional Bach and Beethoven.

We must be careful, however, that we do not become so immersed in developing our children's more obvious, performance-oriented gifts that we neglect to notice and nurture the greater gifts. Gifts such as mercy, persistence, and generosity are often overlooked. Developing our children's character is a much greater task. It is the "heart work" of parenting, and it should be our primary focus.

It was a dark day when my friend Dina's daughter did not get a part in her school play. She was terribly disappointed, feeling shunned by the drama teacher and shocked at being left out of the cast. She had always been assigned lead roles and was normally a prominent part of every production. Despite her confusion and dismay at the results of the auditions, we watched her graciously go to work behind the scenes, working on set design, wardrobe, and being a general gofer for the director. The humility of this fifteen-year-old girl was simply amazing. Indeed, it was a tribute to her mom, who had gently urged her teen to accept the new role God had given her. Keeping a positive outlook, Dina encouraged her daughter to accept the casting call without question and take the opportunity to learn all the things that go into production—things she had never even noticed, things she had taken for granted as an actress.

Reaching a child's heart rests largely on leading by example as a parent. We must be vigilant to model right behavior in our responses to the actions of others—even the curveballs that life throws our way. Then, we applaud our children's efforts to respond as Jesus would. We zero in on His likeness when we show them how volunteerism, loyalty, servanthood, and yes, all the other unnoticed, behind-the-scenes work we do honors the Lord from a heart of true thankfulness. These are real tools that will help them navigate the stormy seas of adolescence.

As our children mature, it is a parent's pain to watch them struggle through the turbulent waters, but it is our joy to watch them grow into the persons that God has custom-designed for His glory and pleasure, focused on becoming more like Christ. By helping them develop their gifts, we are training them in the way they should go and keeping them focused on the fact that God has a plan for their lives.

IDENTIFYING YOUR CHILD'S GIFTS

Encourage interests. Often the very things that are happening in your child's life right now are encouraging him toward God's plan for him. For example, a trip to the emergency room gets your son interested in medicine. Buying a new home has your daughter considering interior design. What are your kids interested in? Find out!

Understand differences. The Lord often pairs an outgoing mother with a shy child (and vice versa). Encourage that child with some behind-the-scenes roles, rather than constantly pushing her into uncomfortable situations. Watch her shine as you assure her of her value and importance.

Get ready to be surprised. Don't be too quick to put your middler into a categorical box. God will reveal timely gifts and attributes; your child will develop new talents and acquire additional interests as he experiences life.

THREE

IMAGE IS EVERYTHING

urt Reynolds, a popular movie star of the seventies, was once interviewed on a daytime talk show. He was sharing with the host that he had just returned from his high school reunion.

"What was that like?" the host inquired.

"It was painful," Burt replied, shaking his head seriously.

"Oh, really?" the host asked, sincerely surprised by his answer. "You had a lot of bad memories?"

"No, not that," Burt answered before cracking a smile. "I had to hold my stomach in all night."

So many of us live and die on appearances. It starts in middle school when we are suddenly surrounded by so many different stages of growth. In elementary days, we may have had race or height to contend with, but now, there is breast development, voice changes, facial hair, and who has permission to shave her legs. It's middle school mayhem! An article in *Time* magazine explains:

Parents are worried about kids growing up faster, and that is physiologically true: 13-year-olds are more mature physically than they were a generation ago. From 1963 to the early 1990s, the age at which a girl got her first period dropped by about one month every decade, to 12.1 years for black girls and 12.6 years for whites. While that may not sound like a lot, says Marcia Herman-Giddens of the University of North Carolina at Chapel Hill, who has been studying the onset of puberty in American children for more than a decade, "there's no evidence that the age of menses has stopped falling. When will it stop? When girls are 9?" There is no consensus about the cause: some scientists blame exposure to certain plastics and insecticides, which degrade into substances with estrogen-related physiological effects. Diets high in meat and protein are associated with earlier puberty. As for boys, Herman-Giddens notes that they are reaching their adult heights at younger ages, which suggests that they too are maturing earlier.

Meanwhile, teens are growing up in a culture that sexualizes children and immerses them in adult images.[6]

Inside, however, they're still kids, kids in adult bodies. Because they are starting to look so grown up, they find that people's expectations of them are changing.

Looks Can Be Deceiving

We base much of our judgment calls on what we see on the

outside. When my son was around eight months old, he was a big baby. He could have easily passed for one year old or older. At church one Sunday, a man looked over at David's baby attempts to crawl toward a toy. "That boy ought to be walking!" he grumped. Fortunately, I didn't have to jump to my son's defense. A friend tartly replied, "That 'boy' is an eight-month-old baby. He is not supposed to be walking!"

And indeed, he wasn't. But looks can be deceiving. And in our show-it-to-me world, looks can be difficult to deal with.

Pat, my mother-in-law, loves to tell the story of how a young, twenty-something butcher at the grocery store wanted a date with her seventh-grade daughter. Karla had developed almost overnight, and she was sporting a woman's height and figure with the immaturity of a giggling girl. The young man's eyes nearly popped out of his head when Pat kindly informed him that the girl he was ogling was just thirteen.

It is the same way with some of our boys. My friend Sandy's son was 5'5" by the time he was eleven years old. To hear her tell it, she put a baby boy to bed one night, his pudgy hands clutching a blanket, and the next morning when she went to wake him, his feet were hanging off the bed. Remarkably, her baby was now taller than she was, bursting through his pj's like the Incredible Hulk. They headed immediately for the mall for new clothes because he needed everything—including underwear. While she was looking in the men's section, torn between boxers or briefs, her son was investigating the underwear rack in the boys' section, torn between Ninja Turtles or Spiderman. He was still a little boy, although he no longer looked like one.

What is it like to be an early adolescent—a child between

the ages of ten and fifteen—a "middler"? It is awkward and embarrassing. It is like running in slow motion toward a finish line that keeps getting moved fifty yards farther out. It is wearing your heart on your sleeve and your attitude on your face. It is walking around wishing you could disappear, be invisible, and just watch life happen to everyone else. It is being in the spotlight onstage when you wish you were in the balcony on the back row.

Middle school circa 1978 was *Star Wars* and *Grease* and the Atari 2600. My friends and I thought we were on the cutting edge. My goal in life was to have a phone in my room, which, when I was fifteen years old, I finally got. It was a chocolate brown slimline (back then, slim was three inches x eight inches). Its rotary dial lit up at night. I thought it was the greatest piece of technology ever.

When I think about what it must be like to be a teen today, I cringe. Internet bullies operate 24/7, and cell phones have cameras, posing the constant threat of life's most embarrassing moment going global in a matter of seconds. I don't know about you, but I do not think I would have lasted.

The mean girls would have had me for lunch. And I would have been so busy devising equally evil ways to squelch them that I would have had no time to study. It was hard enough learning anything as it was! While movies, toys, and technology have upgraded, the war waged on adolescent learning has not. Who can concentrate? For middlers, insecurity still claims that those snickers coming from across the room are personal. Vanity continues to tease the wallflower with dreams that the aimless athlete who is chronically bored in class would change if she were his girlfriend. And for all those on the outside, hope springs eternal that one day, the right outfit, the right remark, the right weather even, might vacate a place in the in crowd.

Out of Reach

In the mid-eighties, "a young, up-and-coming tennis player, sixteen-year-old Andre Agassi, embraced a rebel image. He grew his hair to rocker length, sported an earring, and wore colorful shirts that pushed tennis' still-strict sartorial boundaries. He boasted of a cheeseburger diet and endorsed the Canon *Rebel* camera. *Image is everything* was the ad's line, and it became Agassi's as well."[7] In fact, it became the tagline for a generation already diagnosed with "me-itis."

Today, image remains a primary concern for American youth. Our middle schoolers are moving from the self-centeredness of childhood to the self-consciousness of adolescence. And while they may be having a hard time accepting themselves, they long for other people—their peers, especially—to accept them. For most kids, however, the image they want to convey is far out of their reach.

Girls are driven by prettiness. That's how they judge themselves and each other. Think about the images of beauty and womanhood that are presented to our daughters today, via television, movies, and the Internet. The picture-perfect persona our girls covet is crafted by an entourage of experts: a stylist, a wardrobe person, and a make-up professional. If you have ever watched *American Idol*, you may have seen the evolution of the finalists as they morph into celebrities. Week by week, the contestants are transformed into what a media-driven culture considers beautiful. Bodies are tanned; teeth are bleached; hair is straightened, permed, or extended. How can the average young woman, especially a growing adolescent, compete with that? How can she be content with herself?

I grew up watching the *Brady Bunch* with my big sister. I idolized Marcia and Jan with their spacious home, cute brothers, and long, straight blonde hair. How I coveted their hair! Unfortunately, my wild, frizzy mane was responsible for an image I certainly didn't want to project. I was called "Roseanne Roseannadanna" from day one of middle school. Gilda Radner's character, featured on *Saturday Night Live*, came on way past my bedtime, so I didn't even know who Roseanne Roseannadanna was. In my new school, I was just glad to be getting noticed. I didn't care if the kids called me some goofy, rhyming name. I thought they had made it up. I had no idea it held any significance. In my mind, they were simply greeting me and smiling at me. I was thrilled to be making friends! One Saturday night, however, I couldn't sleep. My sister was watching late-night TV, and I wandered into the den to see what was on. That's when I saw her: Roseanne Roseannadanna. Her wild, dark hair was so like mine. We did look alike. It was obvious why the kids called me that. Stunned, I returned to my room, insulted and hurt.

By the time I graduated from reruns of the *Brady Bunch*, MTV came along. My best friend and I wanted to be like the edgy fashionista Madonna and the powerful rocker Pat Benatar. It seemed there was nothing more important than being cool. Unfortunately, coolness wasn't defined as being the smartest girl in the class. Coolness rotated on an axis of physical beauty and sensuality, and it rested on the acquisition of a boyfriend. Despite several generations' efforts to equate the sexes, for most adolescent girls, times haven't changed. Do-nothing socialites and drug-abusing celebrities make the news far more often than female scientists, researchers, educators, doctors, or lawyers. In this life, cheerleaders will always be more popular than brainiacs.

Consequently, attempts at beauty and celebrity are easily spotted every weekend at the mall. Young girls loiter at the food court, smothered in glittery eye make-up and chatting nervously through lips drenched in shiny gloss. Low-rise jeans hug skinny hips that are just beginning to develop a curve. Navels are exposed where too-tight shirts refuse to tuck in. These girls think they want what the world has to offer. Sucked into a trap of premature sexuality by television, music, and their peers, they sell themselves short for temporary thrills.

Girls at the pivotal ages of twelve and thirteen are making choices that will lay the foundation for the rest of their lives. In the face of the many advances made by our foremothers and the numerous opportunities available for today's women, most girls still base their choices on the deception of a world that appeals to their flesh and their all-consuming need to fit in. And our sons?

Guys are driven by performance. That's how they judge themselves and each other. In fact, guys, too, are willing to go to great lengths in order to achieve the body image they crave: one of physical power and strength.

The world of professional sports, most notably baseball, is a reflection of this drive and the "anything it takes" motivation to succeed. As steroid use has infiltrated the integrity of the game, the trickle-down effect has shown increasing use of these illegal toxins among our teen boys. One father, quoted in *Sports Illustrated*, faced the dilemma head-on with his thirteen-year-old son, a pitching phenom. As a physician, this dad knew exactly what the dangers were. And as a man, this dad knew better than to underestimate the lure performance-enhancing drugs would have on his boy.

> The cheating part doesn't ring a bell with [my son and his friends]. They consider [steroids] no more of an unfair edge than having a better calculator than the kid next to you in math class. I asked if they think it's cheating, and they said, "No, it's just trying to get ahead." The integrity of the game, the old records—that's a non sequitur to these kids. So I tell my son, "Your [testicles] will shrink, you'll get acne. Don't do it, because we don't know what it'll do to you." And I bought the [Jose] Canseco book to show them. All they said when they looked at it was, "Wow, look at the change in Canseco's size!"[8]

According to the Web site of the National Institute on Drug Abuse (NIDA), the trend toward steroid use continues to grow, despite the documented dangers. NIDA director Dr. Alan I. Leshner says, "More than a half million 8th- and 10th-grade students are now using these dangerous drugs, and increasing numbers of high school seniors say they don't believe the drugs are risky."[9]

Driven to succeed in sports, what has happened to our boys' drive to succeed in education? Dove Award-winning recording artist Clay Crosse, in the foreword to *Dig Deep:*

Unearthing the Treasures of Solomon's Proverbs (my Bible study for teen guys), wrote this:

> A recent *Newsweek* magazine cover story was titled, "The Boy Crisis." It described a declining trend with males along every phase of schooling in America. Here were some of the more glaring stats:
>
> - 44% of undergraduate students on college campuses are male. Thirty years ago that number was 58%.
>
> - Boys ages five to twelve are 60% more likely than girls to have repeated at least one grade.
>
> - Eighth grade girls score 21 points higher than boys on standardized writing tests.
>
> - 22% more high school girls are planning to go to college than boys.
>
> These numbers make me sad. As a young man, don't they upset you? Aren't you kind of insulted? They make me ask things like, "Hmmm, are boys really getting dumber, or are girls just getting smarter?" It's a fair question, but truthfully, I don't think either option is true. No one is getting "dumber" and no one is really getting smarter. But clearly, the boys are caring less and less. That can't be denied. These stats are in black and white. They are just numbers but they tell a heartbreaking tale. Something is wrong with the young men and boys of America. They seem to have lost their goals. Their vision. Their purpose.

It's to the point where the kind of young man who has these positive characteristics—clear goals, a focused vision, a definite purpose—is somewhat few and far between. *Rare*. Jesus told us that, "The highway to hell is broad and the gate is wide for the many who choose the easy way. But the gateway to life is small, and the road is narrow, and only a few ever find it."[10]

How do we help our children find it? How can we help them reject the deception of the glamorized image of self? The answer may lie in teaching our children the forgotten virtue of reverence.

Renewing Reverence

As a child, I mostly heard the word *reverence* used in Sunday school by teachers who wanted us kids to sit still for prayer. "Be reverent," they would insist. "Bow your head and close your eyes." Today, the word *reverence* is obsolete. Not only has the word deserted our vocabulary, the virtue itself has gone missing from our culture. Truthfully, reverence is more than simply a posture to be assumed during prayer. Reverence is an attitude to be lived and breathed in our everyday lives.

What is true reverence? One on-line dictionary defined reverence with three meanings: (1) A feeling or attitude of deep respect tinged with awe, (2) the outward manifestation of this feeling: to pay reverence, (3) a gesture indicative of deep respect; an obeisance, bow, or curtsy.

A few years ago, my husband and I were with some friends riding the Long Island ferry across the harbor in New

York City. Most of the people on the ferry boat were commuting from work, something they did night after night. But for us tourists, it was a treat. We were not going to be in New York long enough to enjoy a tour of the Statue of Liberty, but we still wanted to see her as up close as we possibly could. Despite the damp chill in the air, we took the ferry ride just so we could sail by the statue. We huddled out on the deck in our coats and scarves, chattering about all we had seen and done in the city that day. As we drew closer to the great Lady, however, a hush swept over us. Beholding the icon of liberty and justice for all, we were moved to tears. Someone in our group began quietly singing "God Bless America" as we glided by. We all joined hands and sang together, reverently. Indeed, it was a moment of respect tinged with awe as we experienced the knowledge of a deep-rooted sense of patriotism, almost instinctive, and quite bigger than each of us.

In his book, *Reverence: Renewing a Forgotten Virtue,* Paul Woodruff shares this explanation of the feeling and the word itself:

> Reverence begins in a deep understanding of human limitations; from this grows the capacity to be in awe of whatever we believe lies outside our control— God, truth, justice, nature, even death. The capacity for awe, as it grows, brings with it the capacity for respecting fellow human beings, flaws and all. This in turn fosters the ability to be ashamed when we show moral flaws exceeding the normal human allotment.[11]

Adolescence is a season of life that does not exactly foster reverence. Instead, it breeds criticism and comparison within the hearts of our youth. It is a time when even our Christian young people lose sight of their reverence for the Lord. When we lose sight of that, we lose sight of a love for other people. Admittedly, it is hard to love the people who don't love you. It is even more difficult to be faced with the task of loving those who persecute you, ridicule you, and despitefully use you—often on a daily basis. Yet in many instances, that is God's call on the life of a teenager. And if you, the parent, lived through it once, the difficulty is infinitely multiplied when you relive it through your teen.

So is your daughter's Christianity thrown out the window when she begins to be concerned about her appearance? No. Is all hope for a close family trashed when you notice your son is embarrassed by his younger siblings? Not at all. Now is the time to teach your middler the deeper truths of reverence.

Paul Tripp, in his book, *Age of Opportunity: A Biblical Guide for Parenting Teens*, explains that the adolescent years are filled with practical teaching opportunities. "They are the golden age of parenting," he shares, "when you begin to reap all the seeds you have sown in their lives, when you can help your teenager to internalize truth, preparing him or her for a productive, God-honoring life as an adult."[12] Now is the time to shine! Now is the time to embrace every proud hurt, every foolish error, every cross word, and every bad attitude, bringing it under the authority of Christ. Now is the time when the Word is fleshed out in our lives.

Reverence parks on a fear of the Lord, which is the beginning of wisdom. True wisdom then settles on an understanding of self—knowing who you are in right perspective with knowing who God is. It is not the image you project; it is the Christ you reflect. When a young person understands who God is, then who he himself is becomes increasingly well-defined. At a fundamental level, he is enabled to understand that in spite of middle school criteria and culture, everyone is on equal footing. There is a level playing field at the foot of the Cross—no in crowd, no popularity contests, no image save that of Christ alone. From there, everyone is compelled to look up. The love the Savior expressed was meant for all. Out of our gratitude and respect for His wonderful sacrifice, we who are believers must choose to love and honor others, in order that they, too, might come to know Christ Jesus.

What a different world it would be if we could impart that truth to our middlers! And what a different daughter, sister, friend, and student I would have been, way back then, had I been willing to receive this truth. Teach your kids that they are loved and that they belong—to you, of course, but most of all, to the Lord. When they understand they are loved by Him, accepted wholly and completely, then they can pass that love and acceptance on to others.

PRACTICALLY SPEAKING

Proverbial wisdom. Begin reading the Proverbs together. I urge you to buy a Bible translation that your child considers "readable." There are thirty-one chapters in Proverbs, divinely arranged to correspond with the days of the month.

Teach by example. Do you accept the way God made you? Have you gotten over your own teen angst? Are you overly concerned with your own appearance? Do you know what God says about you?

- God says that you are fearfully and wonderfully made (Psalm 139:14).

- God says that you are chosen, holy, and dearly loved (Colossians 3:12).

- God says that you are His child (I John 3:1, 2).

- God says that you are accepted because of your faith in Jesus Christ (Galatians 2:16).

Help where you can. What can you do to help your child with his appearance? With all the hormonal changes, puberty and pimples are one and the same for many kids. Fortunately, today kids don't have to live with acne. There is treatment available in a variety of forms. I had terrible skin problems starting at the age of eleven. I am so thankful that my mother took me to a dermatologist for help. This is something that can and should be treated. It hurts me to see a child who needs treatment and isn't getting it. Some parents believe it is vanity, but I don't. I believe it is doing something to help your child have a better quality of life.

But everyone else does. When your daughter asks to shave her legs, she is probably old enough to do it. I heard one mom sharing about how she had been very hesitant to let her sixth-grade daughter shave her legs. Her daughter, however, had an older brother who came to her defense. "Mom," he explained, "if she's asking, that means everyone else is, and you need to let her do it." I don't know where he got his insight, but the truth is that while a young woman can't do anything about when her period starts or when her figure begins to develop, she can start shaving her legs when everyone else does. And that's okay.

FOUR

CONFRONTING AN
IDOL–DRIVEN CULTURE

S
he was a retired missionary in her sixties, leading a women's Bible study at a large church. My husband and I had just moved our young family to a new city, and I was eager to find my way. I wanted to connect with other Christian moms, and I knew I needed more Bible study, so this weekly class seemed like the perfect fit. One particular morning, the teacher opened our study time with a confession, admitting to a secret sin—an idol in her chaste life. With rapt attention, we listened intently as this quiet, gentle woman revealed that she worshiped pleasure. *Pleasure?* I didn't get it. This was a woman who had spent her life in sacrifice as an overseas missionary. How in the world could she admit to the idol of pleasure?

When she talked about pleasure being an idol in her life, she wasn't referring to some hot, passionate, perverted physical activity that she craved. She wasn't talking about a drug habit, either. In fact, I had difficulty conceiving of her "pleasures" as sin because they were an accepted part of my daily lifestyle. You see, her great admission to our class that day was that she had perched an altar on the pleasures of convenience, laziness, and indifference. Rest and relaxation had reared its ugly, two-pronged head in a life once committed to service and sacrifice. In truth, it was the contemporary American lifestyle of retirement that was bringing this former missionary to her knees. On U.S. soil only a few months and already the enemy tempted her daily with the forbidden fruit of what we would call "the good life."

As moms today we find ourselves living in a culture that advocates the merits of pleasure, selfishness, and materialism. Integrity is viewed as outdated; abstinence is deemed overrated, and servanthood is considered antiquated at best. The world's greatest leaders scoff at the idea of moral character and expect to be easily excused from their errors. Sports heroes no longer care to be role models, disregarding their young fans as they abandon self-control and give in to red-hot tempers and red-blooded passions. Modern-day America's best-loved teenage sweethearts frantically ditch their Gidget-like girlness to become vampish divas—flaunting their sexuality by the ripe old age of fifteen.

Challenge the Status Quo

Enter the Christian home. We are called to set up housekeeping in this world while remaining separate from its way of life. Many of us moms spent our teens and early twenties ensnared in the sinful lifestyle we now abhor. How do we raise kids who confront the culture and challenge the status quo for Christ?

In her book, *The Power of a Praying Parent*, author Stormie Omartian writes, "At every stage of their lives our children need and will greatly benefit from our prayers."[13] Even as we are committed to providing physical nourishment for our children, we should be as devoted to praying for their spiritual needs. We wouldn't think of going a day without feeding our kids; in fact, we are diligent to see that they don't miss a meal! Yet when it comes to praying for them, we can be so casual. Prayer is the sharpest knife in the drawer! It is the only tool that truly wields power in raising children who confront the culture for Christ. Prayer should be a mother's daily work.

While there are cookbooks and cable channels that offer recipes galore for feeding your family, as well as appliances to take care of the hard job of preparing it, how can we learn to effectively pray for our kids? The Bible offers several prayer warriors as examples, and I have a favorite in Epaphras, an itinerant preacher and missionary who, along with Paul, was imprisoned for preaching the Gospel. In a letter to the Christians of the church at Colossae,[14] Paul mentioned that Epaphras was faithful to pray for them. In fact, he said that Epaphras "labored in prayer." The Greek word Paul used meant that Epaphras struggled or fought—as one might contend with an adversary[15]—in prayer as he pleaded with God for those new Christians to mature in their faith. How do you learn to pray like that?

When Jesus taught the disciples about prayer, He told them to enter a closet and close the door for serious prayer time.[16] In truth, it is somewhat difficult to find a prayer closet in a prison cell. Paul and Epaphras were chained, arms and legs bound, crouching side by side in jail. During their imprisonment, Paul had heard Epaphras praying. He had seen him go to bat before the throne of God, interceding on behalf of his "kids," the Colossian Christians, whom he had introduced to Jesus. Paul couldn't help this intrusion, nor could Epaphras do anything less revealing. Circumstances dictated that in the absence of a prayer closet, there were two choices: Either don't pray at all, or pray openly to the only One who has a full view of the heart.

Sadly, and much to my shame, there are days when I look at my circumstances and don't see the possibility of a prayer closet. My prison cell is curtained off by the snooze button, guarded by a schedule that has no margin, and my arms and legs are bound by the chains of late-night TV. However, if I am to learn anything from Epaphras, it is this: It is vital that my children stand firm in their faith, mature and fully assured.[17] This is the prayer that couldn't wait for a prayer closet. This was Epaphras's prayer from a prison cell. He wanted his spiritual children to continue growing in their faith. He didn't want to see them languish at the edge of their relationship with Christ, content with knowing Him as Savior, yet hesitant to explore a deeper walk. And isn't that every Christian's struggle? It's our struggle; it's our kids' struggle. Epaphras was greatly aware of the fact that anything less than constant growth meant the enemy was gaining ground. So he labored in prayer. He worked at it. And Paul was witness to real struggle, as the powers of darkness fought against the fervent prayers of one righteous, praying man who was able to shrug off his circumstances and stand in the gap for his "kids."

Truthfully, praying isn't all that difficult. If you can talk, you can pray. But like any other form of speech, there are variations on the theme. If you want a promotion at work, you plan what you are going to say to your boss. You think about it; you psych yourself up, and you don't go for it unless you are really sure you want it. When the day comes that you find yourself in conference with your boss, you hear yourself passionately explaining why you want what you want. Perhaps, when it comes to praying for our kids, we are not exactly passionate because we are not exactly sure what we want.

My friend Mark once shared with me that he had been praying for God to show him his children's weaknesses. He figured then he would know how best to pray for them. Wryly, he admitted that in praying this, God had also shown him his own frailties. The same goes for me. Often the things I notice as trouble spots for my children are things I contend with myself. If I want to raise children who put others first, then that's the kind of person I need to be. If I want my children to show self-control, then I need to be self-controlled. If I want my children to love God with all their hearts, souls, and minds, then I must exemplify that passion in my own life. I have to really want it for myself in order to really want it for them. Epaphras certainly set the example for the Colossians. His was a risky, life-or-death approach to faith, worth staking life and all its idols on.

Taken by Surprise

In the alphabetical order of my school days, I spent many years sitting in front of Steve Irving[18] in homeroom. One morning,

Steve was very busy "engraving" something on his wooden desk. Using a ballpoint pen, he carefully etched "Steve Irving is #1." When he showed me his handiwork before we left for classes, I could tell that Steve was very proud of his work. Steve was a fine athlete and a good-looking guy, not to mention easy-going and friendly. He must have thought that his modest announcement would be met with agreement by the people who would be sitting at his desk in classes throughout the day. Not so!

When we returned to homeroom the next morning, "Steve Irving is #1" had become "Steve Irving is #100." The next day he was #1000. By the end of the week, the zeros had become so numerous that someone had inserted commas in order to make sense of it all. Steve Irving had become number one bazillion. Poor Steve was truly astonished. He couldn't believe anyone would argue with his little declaration. He never thought he had any enemies.[19]

In the New Testament, the apostle Peter clearly cautioned new believers to be self-controlled and alert; he warned them of their enemy, the devil, who prowls around like a roaring lion looking for someone to devour.[20] Despite warnings throughout Scripture, however, Christian parents are often shocked when Satan attacks, especially when he attacks their kids. They are not prepared; their children are not prepared. They are taken by the element of surprise and, in most cases, not ready to do battle.

For example, as Americans, we worship the idol of youth. Youth is synonymous with beauty. And somehow, youth and beauty have become synonyms for wisdom. Our kids are surrounded by media images of teen celebrities and recording artists who are depicted as wiser, more savvy, and, in general, more together than their adult counterparts. They are deceived into thinking that kids are on equal footing with their parents. When was the last time you saw a functional family on television? You know, one where the parents have authority and the children respect, trust, and obey them? The Bradys, Waltons, and Huxtables are available only in reruns.

God's umbrella of protection begins with Him—God over all—but then Dad steps up as the head of the household, followed by Mom, and finally the children. What happens when children step out from under that umbrella? In the hurricane of adolescence, they are going to get drenched. Even in ancient times, King Solomon solemnly warned his own son about the foolishness of being wise in his own eyes.[21]

In a perverted twisting of God's best plan, young people—those with the least amount of life experience, those with the least education, those with the least amount of insight and maturity—see themselves as virtual fountains of knowledge and authenticity! What's worse, they are encouraged in this view. Teens are portrayed as all-knowing and all-powerful on television shows, movies, and Internet hotspots. At the same time, in these same media offerings, the parents interact and relate with the kids as peers—well-intentioned, but sadly misinformed—peers. Not wise instructors. Not respected elders. They are either absent, distracted, or idiotic. This is backwards. It totally undermines God's order of the family and the position of the parents as supervisory. Instead, young people are elevated to unearned heights from which they will inevitably fall. Real wisdom, real knowledge, begins with the fear of the Lord. Knowing who God is and having a reverence for Him encourages the virtue of modesty. Modesty is best described by what it is not: It is not flamboyant, boastful, or self-centered. It is quiet, unassuming, and knows its place. Modesty is a representation of self that seeks to present a servant attitude to God and others.

Now Comes the Hard Part

When my youngest was born, it was a difficult delivery. The nurses were talking openly about the intense moments before and after Derek's birth as they wrapped up their paperwork in my birthing suite. One of them came over to check on me and said, "You can relax; he's safe and sound. The hard part is over."

I smiled and gently replied, "Oh, no. The hard part will be raising him to be a godly man in an ungodly world." For believing parents everywhere, the real labor begins after delivery. But the questions? The questions begin at conception, and sometimes even before.

The Old Testament story of the birth of Samson begins with an angelic visitation to Samson's soon-to-be expectant mom.[22] The angel explains to her that she will become pregnant with a son who is to be a Nazirite, set apart to God from birth. Nazirites had strict dietary regimens to follow, which the angel explained that she (the mom) would have to follow as well. When his wife tells him about the angel's visit, Samson's soon-to-be expectant dad, Manoah, gets a little bit anxious. Since he missed out, he wants the angel to return, and so he prays, "O Lord, I beg You, let the man of God You sent to us come again to teach us how to bring up the boy who is to be born" (Judges 13:8, NIV). Although centuries have passed, all new parents echo Manoah's heartfelt request: Somebody, tell me how to do this!

Here's what happened. God allowed the angel to return, but his words were not some epiphany of dos and don'ts. He simply told Manoah that his wife must do everything he had told her to do. You see, he told her to follow the dietary regimen of a Nazirite because he knew it would ensure that the baby would do the same. His advice for child-raising was simple and practical: Do what you want the baby to do. Or in this case, do what God wants the baby to do. God wanted a baby who was set apart, who would grow into a man who was set apart. His instructions were given to a mom who had to be set apart as well. In that Near East ancient culture as well as today's global electronic world, a person sets herself apart by the choices she makes.

Motivating Modesty

There are more idols. The idols of convenience, habit, and appearance deceive our children on a daily basis. Their influence can be best explained by the lure of the drive-thru window. You see, the success of the drive-thru window is due largely to convenience, habit, and appearance working together. It is extremely *convenient* to pick up a sandwich. Millions of people pick up a breakfast sandwich every day on the way to work; thus, it becomes a *habit*. The drive-thru has a beautiful, full-color sign, and the parking lot is clean. The window itself is sparkling. It has a pleasant *appearance*.

Most people don't stop to think about the consequences of their choices. In the case of the daily drive-thru customer, she isn't thinking about the fact that her tasty bacon, egg, and cheese biscuit comes loaded with fat grams, cholesterol, and sodium. This adds up to a poor health habit that will not be convenient when it manifests itself in physical problems later on.

Likewise, the enemy longs to render your child completely useless in the kingdom of God. He approaches our middlers with the same tactics he has used since Adam and Eve. He asks them to come and admire the forbidden, dressing it up with glamour and fun. Then he tells them they can have it; it is theirs for the taking, and no one ever needs to know. Most middlers don't stop to think about the consequences of their choices, and, like Eve, they bite.

I spent my middle and high school years submerged in the 1980s. The rampant materialism of the day was like an IV in the arm of idolatry. The media was not as far-reaching then, but through movies, television, pop music, and fashion magazines, it still managed to erect idols in my soul: the idol of glamour, the forbidden, foolish vanity, and unwarranted pride. I had an enemy! And I still do. As parents, we must warn our children of the enemy and help them defeat him, first by surrendering our own idols, and then by developing a daily battle plan.

Making a decision for Christ opposes the idols of the world. It confronts the culture with His truth, taking on many forms in order to reach all people with His message. When you receive too much change and give it back to the store clerk, when you befriend a stranger, when you overlook a wrong, and when you pray for those who hurt you, you are confronting the culture. But does that make a real difference? It can potentially make a life or death difference, if, as the apostle Peter taught, you are "ready to speak up and tell anyone who asks why you're living the way you are, and always with the utmost courtesy" (1 Peter 3:15b, Msg). We can challenge the way things are by choosing the way God meant them to be. We can be set apart, and so can our kids.

Confronting the idols in our modern-day culture means choosing a lifestyle that is set apart—not one that is tucked away. We must live boldly according to God's precepts, engaging a people who are desperate for His abundant life, showing them a different way to go. Our children need to see that alternate route as well. They will best resist the pull of the world if they are standing firm on right choices—choices they have learned to make, one after the other, over their growing-up years.

The last thing your middler needs is a religion full of don'ts. He needs a relationship with Jesus Christ—a personal connection that is as integral to everyday decisions as it is to life's major crossroads. Truly, the middle school years are a time when the everyday decisions seem like major crossroads. What to wear, what band to listen to, what friends to hang out with—these are all monumental moments in the life of a middler. Because of their desperate need for peer approval, coupled with their desire to blend in, many kids will go along with the crowd because it's the easy thing to do. The idol of convenience tempts them to take the easy way out, so *fitting in* and going along with the crowd is far easier than *thinking through* and taking a stand provoked by conviction. As parents, we must teach our kids how to navigate the multitude of choices the world presents. We have to help them learn how to think through things. For example, if your child begins to show an interest in a secular band that doesn't meet your approval, find a similar Christian band and purchase their CDs. Then begin asking the tough questions. If it is the type of music that was appealing (country, rock, hip-hop), the problem is solved. But if it is the band's worldliness, their lyrics, or their lifestyle that your teen found attractive, you need to find out why—and your child, also, needs to confront his attraction to sin.

Ginger Plowman, in her book, *Don't Make Me Count to Three!*, explains that the most productive form of communication is learning how to draw out the thoughts of another. [23] She writes, "When you help your child to understand what is in his heart, you are teaching him to evaluate his own motives, which will help to equip him for his walk with Christ as he grows into an adult." To find out what is going on in your child's heart, Ginger recommends asking heart-probing questions with a threefold approach.

- You must learn to help your child express what she is thinking.

- You must learn to help your child express how she is feeling.

- You must learn how to discern matters of the heart from actions and words.

If your child is becoming brand-conscious, use the opportunity for a shopping trip that explores brand names, discount stores, and the trap of credit cards. If she still wants the name brand, let her pay for the difference in cost between it and a similar off brand. But don't let her off the hook without asking the right questions! Probe her heart with inquiries such as:

- Why is it important to have the name brand?

- Is someone teasing you about the clothes you wear?

- Is there something that you want people to know about you that a certain manufacturer's label says better than your actions say?

Follow-up questions are equally important. Once the decision is made, what is the outcome? When it comes to bands, there are Christian groups existing as alternatives in almost every genre. In the case of clothing, my daughter quickly found out that much of the exclusive name-brand items are lacking in quality. Be sure to follow up in those particular instances with questions that help your child decide if the financial investment was worth it.

Toolbox

GOING AGAINST THE FLOW

New heroes. Read biographies or watch videos of Christians who made a difference in the world by taking a stand for Christ. Try Eric Liddell ("Chariots of Fire"), Jim Elliot, and Corrie ten Boom.

Family ratings. Establish entertainment guidelines to help your child know what is appropriate and what is not.

Spin it. Select age-appropriate news items and give your child a Christian perspective on current events.

Think twice. Work against a throw-away mentality by repairing items instead of replacing them.

· · · · ·

FIVE

ACTIVELY INVOLVED PARENTS

hen Danya was two, we left her in the care of her grandparents as we went out for dinner with Rich's boss, Howard, and his wife. They had left their twelve- and fourteen-year-old daughters home alone. Listening to Howard worry about everything from the girls having their friends over to the pizza delivery guy being a psychopath left me feeling much better about the parenting demands I was then facing on a daily basis. Sure, there was a great deal of "hands-on" in my life as a mom, but watching Howard deal with the "hands-off" aspect made me feel like I was enjoying the easier years!

As our children enter middle school, much of the exhausting, debilitating part of parenting is over. Our children are largely self-sufficient, and many parents begin to shift their attention to what they believe to be more pressing concerns. Our kids' adolescent years often come along at a time when we are entering a busier stage of life. Some of us moms go back to work. We may begin experiencing health problems as we grow older. Our own parents are often entering a season of life when they begin needing more of our attention to meet their health and aging needs. Financial pressures arise as we begin to think about college tuition costs. In short, even the best, most involved hands-on parents can get distracted. Yet these are the years when intentional parenting, being actively involved with your child, is essential. How can you stay connected?

The Family Table

Let's start with the family table. Is it a reality or a dream at your house? Finding the time to plan and produce a meal night after night can be difficult. However, statistics show that the family table may very well be critical to your child's health and emotional well-being—quite possibly the most effective weapon in the war on drugs. Writer Joseph A. Califano, Jr. found the odds that twelve- to seventeen-year-olds will smoke, drink, or use marijuana rise as the number of meals they have with their parents declines. Only six percent of kids who eat dinner with their parents six or more times a week smoke compared with twenty-four percent of those who eat dinner with their parents twice a week or less; for marijuana use, it's twelve percent compared with thirty-five percent.[24]

According to Leanne Ely, author of *Saving Dinner*, statistics like these remind her that eating dinner together is worth any inconvenience and energy it may take to pull it off. "I consider the family table sacred," she says.[25]

The Judeo-Christian culture is founded upon a variety of traditions and rituals that involve food. From the earliest recorded celebrations in the Bible, food has played an important part in feasting and fun. Today's culture is no different in this respect. Food plays a huge role in our lives, from weddings to wakes. Unfortunately, we sometimes downplay the importance of food in the daily life of a family. Leanne explains that parents must look at each day as being the cornerstone of a child's life, not just the celebrations. "The celebrations are planned, but it's day-to-day life that impacts our kids."

Day-to-day life, however, is full of activities. By the time evening rolls around, many families are divided not only by parents' work schedules, but also by the kids' activities, such as sports practices, music lessons, or dance rehearsals. My friend Kathy Fletcher, a mother of two in Charlotte, North Carolina, candidly admits, "Every step of the family table is difficult, from planning and shopping to cooking and cleaning up. We are slightly overextended." Leanne explains that it is precisely because of our hectic lifestyles that we need the family table. "There needs to be a place where we can sit down, take a breath and say, 'Whew! How was your day?'"

The family table is not an impossibility but an investment. You are investing your time and resources into the people you love the most! How can it happen in your home? Get your family together to ask them for some of their favorite meals. Put together twelve menu ideas (these will serve as a two-week rotation of dinner meals), and create a master grocery list. These meals do not have to be elaborate. Choose things everybody likes that you feel confident creating. Once you make that initial investment of your time, take five minutes a week to check your calendar to determine which nights the family table would be the most doable. (Incorporate a pizza night when you need to, and enjoy delivery, take-out, or store-bought around your table.) Take an additional ten minutes to put together a shopping list from your master.

"When we take the family dinner table and look at it with different eyes, we understand that it's going to have an impact on our children's future. It represents security, a place where they can come and talk about their day and know that somebody is going to take time to listen to them," concludes Leanne. "If we do that, we've accomplished much."

Toolbox

A RECIPE FOR SUCCESS

Pre-heat. If you haven't established a family dinnertime, begin with a couple of nights a week.

Keep it simple. Utilize a Crock-Pot so that dinner is ready when you get home in the evening. These recipes are widely available on the Internet.

Stir. Get your kids involved in the process. They can make the salad, set the table, and pour the drinks. They can help clean up afterwards, too.

Soup's on. Be sure to have at least one item even your picky eater will eat.

Lick the bowl. Remember to make it fun!

Family Meetings

Kim, a teacher and mother of three, recognizes the two tell-tale signs that her family isn't connecting. First, their schedule is full, with no down time. It's difficult to juggle the sports schedules, school assignments, and church activities of her busy children. She and her husband tag team in order to get each one where he or she needs to be, but at times even the most careful planning doesn't dismiss a flustered feeling of hurriedness in their lives. Second, with the family going in different directions, stress causes behavior problems to erupt. "That's when we'll have a family meeting to sit down and discuss where we're going as a family," Kim explains. "It helps us keep our focus on what's important."

What business or corporation could function without regular meetings? Family meetings, when integrated regularly into family life, present a safe, loving environment that fosters open communication and affection between family members. When it's time for a family meeting, it's time for talking, planning, teaching, and loving—together.

"At our house, family meetings are a time when everyone comes together around the kitchen table to make sure we are all on the same page," says Melissa Taylor, a mother of four in Charlotte, North Carolina. "We meet once or twice a month, usually on a Sunday night."

Some families may opt to use their meeting time to discuss particular issues relevant to the ages of their children, such as the dangers of substance abuse or the importance of establishing priorities. It is important to maintain openness; no topic should be off-limits, and everyone should get a chance to talk.

"We really believe in having meetings and asking questions," says Tom Elliff, author of the book, *Unbreakable: The Seven Pillars of a Kingdom Family.*[26] He and his wife, Jeannie, have four grown children and twenty grandchildren. They advise families not to wait until there is a crisis situation to have a meeting.

"Making decisions as a family in a calm, non-critical situation allows those decisions to become like a compass when the sea becomes turbulent," Tom explains. "There may be a lot of different things going on, but the child still has his compass: those decisions."

Kim and her husband let their kids help every year in planning the family's vacation. "Jimmy and I wanted to drive cross-country to the Grand Canyon this year." Kim smiles. "After our family meeting, we decided to wait a couple more years before attempting it." Their family meeting revealed that Kim and Jimmy's three children had other ideas for vacation. The oldest had her heart set on a trip to Colonial Williamsburg. One of their sons wanted to go the beach, and the other one was rooting for a trip to a major league baseball game. Kim admits that if they had not held a family meeting, she and Jimmy would have spent their vacation funds on a trip the two of them were interested in, but one that held no attraction for their children. Family meetings encourage a team atmosphere in the home, giving the kids an opportunity for their suggestions and comments to be heard.

While there are times for group discussion, children must realize the final verdict rests squarely on their parents. There are some decisions in life that children are not equipped to make. The parents must take the responsibility for those critical choices.

Besides vacation planning, family meetings can be a time for helping everyone focus on the day, week, or month ahead. The Elliffs held informal family meetings every morning around the breakfast table when their kids were teens. They found that a morning meeting set a positive tone for the day ahead. "At breakfast time, everybody's fresh," Tom acknowledges. "In the evenings, a family meeting can come off as a sort of damage report."

Another advantage of morning meetings is that the family avoids the distractions of phone calls or friends dropping by. "I had a huge calendar with everyone's activities posted on it," Jeannie Elliff remembers. Every morning, the calendar was consulted in order to incorporate a greater sense of connection between the four siblings. Everyone knew what was going on and where each family member would be that day.

"As the kids get older and our schedule gets more and more packed, the family meeting helps us all know what is needed, where we are going, what we can and can't do, and how to do it all," agrees Melissa. "It helps our family to function as a team instead of six people with six lives living under the same roof."

Family meetings are ripe with teaching opportunities, giving children real-life lessons on marriage, manners, and other family matters. When the parents present a united front before their children, they teach unity, the bedrock of marriage. "Never disagree in front of the children," advises Jeannie. "Every child has a 'divide and conquer' agenda! If they can get their parents to divide on an issue, then one of the parents has to give in. This sets a terrible example." The Elliffs avoided splitting on issues by meeting together, just the two of them, every morning before meeting with the kids.

"We were in agreement before the kids even got up," remarks Tom. "We wanted them to see that for one parent to speak, it was the same as both parents speaking."

Family meetings offer a time to prepare children for life events. When Melissa's grandmother passed away, she and her husband, Jeff, used the safe setting of a family meeting to prepare their children for the sights and sounds of a funeral and a grieving family. Keep in mind that if you have several children in a wide age span, there may be times when you hold family meetings after the little ones are tucked in bed. Debriefing the older kids when Dad loses his job or when Mom needs surgery is imperative before couching the situation in easier terms for the younger children.

For celebration and encouragement, family meetings provide a perfect backdrop. This is a great time to honor good grades, wise decisions, and personal accomplishments. Meeting together provides an occasion to affirm each other in additional ways as well. Melissa recalls a special family meeting that her son Blake once called. The family dog had run away, and Melissa blamed herself because she was the one who had left the gate open. The family gathered to comfort her and let her know they didn't think it was her fault. Blake made a special card for her, and everyone assured her that God had a purpose and a plan for the way things had happened. "That particular meeting was the turning point for me in that situation. Our family roles were reversed. The wisdom and truth I have tried to teach my kids was returned to me when I needed it."

Combine your family meetings with family fun. Serve special snacks, or hold your family meeting at a park or favorite restaurant. Establish a tradition of communication, respect, and love through a time for regular family meetings.

Toolbox

PLANNING A FAMILY MEETING

Kickoff. The right Bible passage can enhance your meeting when you choose one that relates to the issue being discussed. Prayer softens hearts and smoothes edgy attitudes, preparing everyone with a spirit of peace.

The goal. Parents should have a definite agenda for the meeting. Stay on task so the meeting accomplishes its objective. Tag someone as "secretary" and keep a list of minutes.

Advance the ball. Every meeting should include a time for open discussion. Allow the children to make comments or bring up issues that are important to them.

Playing time. Determine the length of your meetings in accordance with the age of your children. Young children will find a lengthy meeting difficult.

Roughing the kicker. Establish rules of speech: no name-calling and no sarcasm.

Interference. Keep everyone focused on the meeting by

eliminating the distractions of TV, radio, and telephone calls.

Personal foul. If a family member brings a complaint to the meeting, they must also have at least one solution in mind to remedy the situation.

Holding. Every meeting should close in prayer, with hugs all around!

Dating Your Child

My husband and I met in college. We were good friends and often saw each other in group settings before we started dating. Once he asked me out, however, I looked forward to some time spent away from the noise of the crowd. I wanted to know more about his background, his thoughts, his likes and dislikes. I relished the idea of a quiet dinner focused on getting to know him.

Now that I'm a mother, I realize it is essential to spend time focusing on my children one at a time. Of course, I know my children's background and history information, but as they rapidly grow and change, I want to know the persons they are becoming. I have found that a great way to connect with my kids is to get away occasionally for some one-on-one time, otherwise known as a date! Don't worry—this does not have to be expensive! Dating your kids operates on the same philosophy you may remember from your own dating days: It's not about money. It's about spending time together.

When I was an elementary student, my dad drove me to

school and picked me up every day. It was a twenty-minute trip each way, and during that time I had my dad's undivided attention. We talked. We sang. We made up games. I remember some of the silliest conversations we had. One day I told him I wanted to be Miss Tennessee, the next day, the President of the United States. He was an attentive listener and encouraged me always in my walk with the Lord. Every Friday afternoon, we celebrated the weekend by stopping for an Icee. Those special times with my dad are some of my best memories of childhood—simple, unhurried moments together. Times like these are especially important to a middler. When we moved and I started riding the bus as a sixth-grader, I really missed those rides with my dad.

Individual time spent with your child provides a safe atmosphere for discussing important issues. Things that would never come up at the family dinner table often surface in the confidential confines of a car or a restaurant's corner booth. During her two children's school days, my friend Mary often picked one or the other up an hour or two early for a date. "It was a time of catching up on what was going on *inside*," she recalls. "It was amazing how many serious issues were first revealed on those dates."

I love grabbing one of my kids and conning them into going to the grocery store with me. It doesn't take much cajoling anymore because it always turns into a date. My grocery day used to be Friday mornings. While my older two were usually trying to be sure they had completed all their school assignments for the week, my youngest had his work finished and was always ready to tag along with Mom. We left early and hit a fast food place for a biscuit and a soft drink (special occasion!), and we would sit in the van in the parking lot of the market, talking and enjoying our breakfast. That went on for weeks until one of the older ones asked why Derek never ate breakfast before leaving for the grocery store with me—then the jig was up!

I once interviewed Michelle Duggar, the phenomenal Arkansas mom of seventeen children whose family has been featured on the Discovery Channel. I asked her if she managed to have any of that all-important one-on-one time with her children. If I find I must be purposeful in planning dates with each of my three, how in the world does Michelle do it with seventeen? When it comes to quality time, she credits the decision to homeschool as being the best thing for her large family. It's what enables Michelle and her husband, Jim Bob, to spend a great deal of time together, day in and day out, with their children. But she also uses a unique system for creating special moments with each child. She explains:

> When I'm working with one of them on spelling words, we may spend thirty minutes to an hour just on one spelling test, getting ready for it and all that. There are so many opportunities to communicate, especially when they're getting wiped out and frustrated over the words. It gives us time to talk about heart issues. I'll ask, "Why are you so stressed out? What's going on?" There may be some conflict with another sibling that they haven't resolved, and we need to walk through it. I think we have a lot of opportunities like that, just because of the dynamics of homeschooling. I'm here with them all the time.
>
> Also, I keep two lists. The children made a

chart for the little ones who are eight years old and younger. If I'm running an errand to the post office or something quick like that, the little ones get a turn, one-on-one with Mommy. The first thing we're talking about as we're driving out the driveway is, "What's on your mind? Got anything you want to talk to Mommy about?" Some of them are really talkative, and they never stop from the time we leave the house! But others, I have to pull it out of them. So I specifically ask, "Tell me about this or that, or how do you feel about this or that?"

The older ones take turns helping me with the bigger tasks, like grocery shopping for the fresh stuff, which I do around every three days. Those older ones still want to go with me. They still want that one-on-one time with me. We talk the whole time we're gone.

Because of his real estate business, Jim Bob is here quite a bit, and he often takes them one-on-one with him to show property. I imagine that my children, when they talk about what they liked the most or the things they really enjoyed, will bring up that one-on-one time with me or their dad.[27]

Dates are a great time for enjoying yourself with your child. Laugh at your teen's randomness and silly stories about her friends. Share some funny stories from your own growing-up years. Always remember to keep a positive tone to your dates. Your objective is to build the relationship. Dennis Rainey, president of FamilyLife, agrees. "I would take my daughters shopping, which is the equivalent of taking my sons hunting," says Rainey, laughing. "My daughters like to bag a clothing item or two, and I like to spoil them a bit. It was always a battle, though, to take them shopping because as clothing has become more and more immodest, I had to be careful that the shopping date didn't turn out negative and undermine the very relationship I was seeking to build."[28]

Dates don't have to be elaborate. A stroll in the park can be just as memorable as going to a sporting event. The bottom line is that we date our children for the same reasons we dated (and hopefully, continue to date!) our spouses: for uninterrupted, quality time together and for the chance to get an up-close view of the person God is developing. Life charges on at a hectic pace. A date with your child is like pressing the pause button. Press it, Mom! Press it again and again! Make those dates a priority.

Toolbox

BE A GREAT DATE

Be attentive. Focus on your child. No cell phones or beepers allowed!

Be considerate. Keep in mind your child's age and interests when choosing activities.

Be there. Do it together, whether it's climbing the rock wall or playing mini golf.

Be creative. Never underestimate the element of surprise.

Be on time. Keep the appointments you make with your child.

Be real. Share your heart with your child.

Be thankful. Pray with your child before and after your date.

SIX

FRIENDS VERSUS ACQUAINTANCES

When my daughter was eleven, she became friends with Mandy,[29] a twelve-year-old who faced a lot of challenges in life. Mandy's parents had divorced when her father "came out" and told her mother that he wanted to live an openly homosexual lifestyle. From that point on, Mandy began to live a sort of double life, as do many children of divorce who must split their time between their moms and dads. Mandy's double life, however, came with two contrasting environments. She spent the bulk of her time in her mother and stepfather's Christian home, but she spent every other weekend with her dad and his partner in a God-defying atmosphere. On the occasions when Mandy was at home on the weekend, she would often visit in our home on Sunday afternoon, or Danya would go home with her after church. They were getting to be pretty good friends when Danya asked if Mandy could spend the night sometime.

Knowing how impressionable my daughter was at eleven, knowing she might not understand what I was about to tell her, and knowing also that she might get upset with me, I explained to her that Mandy was not a "spend-the-night friend." You see, it was time for me to explain to my daughter the difference between intimate friends and acquaintances, and in order to put it into a context I knew she would be able to understand, I coined a new Powell family term.

At that time, Mandy could not be a spend-the-night friend because spend-the-night friends had to be kids that I knew well and trusted. After all, try as I might to stay up late, I eventually have to turn in. When there are kids in the house awake, and I'm asleep, that is unsupervised time. Girls share all kinds of secrets and become more vulnerable in direct proportion to the later it gets, from midnight on. It's a time when, whether you want to believe it or not, the enemy can gain ground in our children's thoughts and attitudes. In this particular example, Mandy, like any daughter, loved her daddy; in her eyes, he could do no wrong. She had been overexposed and thus desensitized to the homosexual lifestyle, loving and acknowledging his male partner as her stepparent. This was her life's version of normal. During a critical season when I was laying a foundation of right and wrong concerning God's Word and sexuality, Mandy was a twelve-year-old messenger of propaganda. She did not need total access to my daughter's impressionable mind. While she was more than welcome in our home, it was only going to be when I was awake.

If you don't realize the pull your children's friends will have on their lives, please consider this chapter a wake-up call. Peer pressure is alive and well, and much of peer influence is simply a fact of life at this age. In the pre-teen and teenage years, friendships become especially important. It is crucial for your middler to understand that his true friend-ships need to be built around like-minded people with similar values. These are the friends who will influence his life! Like it or not, if you're honest with yourself, you will admit that many of the things your friends said and did when you were growing up affected who you are today. Their words are writ-ten on some of the deepest places in your heart. If you want to understand the effect of peer influence on your child's life, please don't be guilty of underestimating the monstrous pull of the crowd and the mammoth appeal of peer approval.

Ah, friends. The word itself meant something entirely different just a decade ago, but in today's global society, our kids have tons of "friends" at their fingertips, courtesy of the computer. *Business Week* magazine recently tagged today's kids as the "MySpace generation" or "Generation @."[30]

> Although networks are still in their infancy, experts think they're already creating new forms of social behavior that blur the distinctions between online and real-world interactions. In fact, today's young generation largely ignores the difference. Most adults see the Web as a supplement to their daily lives. They tap into information, buy books or send flowers, exchange apartments, or link up with others who share passions for dogs, say, or opera. But for the most part, their social lives remain rooted in the tra-ditional phone call and face-to-face interaction.
>
> The MySpace generation, by contrast, lives comfortably in both worlds at once. Increasingly,

America's middle- and upper-class youth use social
networks as virtual community centers, a place to go
and sit for a while (sometimes hours).

When it comes to middle schoolers and social networking,
these on-line sites present multiple challenges for parents. Let
common sense prevail as you work your way around these
sites (see toolbox), establishing rules for your middler. That
part isn't really all that difficult. What I see as a greater challenge is helping kids understand the true meaning of the word
"friend" in contrast to multiple listings of strangers. A picture
and a list of trivial facts about a person do not constitute the
makings of a friendship. Communicating with someone on-
line, even for an extended period of time, does not equal the
knowledge that results from a "live and in person" friendship.
These on-line "friends" are acquaintances at best.

Triple-A Friendships

In her book, *The Power of a Praying Parent*, Stormie Omartian
acknowledges God's Word as clearly instructing Christians
not to be unequally yoked together with unbelievers.[31] "That
doesn't mean our children can never have a non-believ-
ing friend," she writes. "But there is clear implication that
their closest friends, the ones to whom they have strong ties,
should be believers."[32] When it comes to these relationships,
I want my children to understand their true friends are the
ones who can be counted on for three things: accountability,
advice, and authenticity. These qualities set the standard for
a triple-A friendship.

Accountability has become somewhat of a buzzword

among Christians, especially among men's and women's small groups. If we are not careful, our children will get the impression that accountability is an adult thing, when it is really a Christian thing.

Accountability simply means to be held answerable for accomplishing a goal, completing a task, or even behaving in a certain way. In our Christian circles, it can mean that one is held responsible for the knowledge she has gained. For example, if your pastor preaches on tithing one Sunday morning, you are then accountable to act like a person who has learned about tithing. Having learned what God's Word says about that financial principle, you are expected to act on it. As a Christian, you are accountable to apply those biblical truths to your life.

In the same way, our kids need to understand that in close Christian friendships, accountability has the right to ask questions.

Why did you do that?

Accountability has the permission to confront.

Dude, she is your sister! Don't treat her that way!

Accountability has the privilege to probe.

Why don't you like playing with your little brother? He just wants to hang around us.

Accountability in a friendship must exist to tackle the hard questions as both people are called higher in relationship with Christ.

As children grow into middlers, they will be approaching their friends more and more with their various problems and life issues. This doesn't mean that they won't be coming to you, Mom! It just means they will also be turning to their friends. They need to be choosing friends who can provide them with trustworthy counsel and good, solid advice.

At this age, also, our kids begin to turn to other adults for friendships. They begin asking the adults they admire and respect for their take on the different situations that come up in their lives. How do you feel about the youth minister at your church? What about the Sunday school teachers? These are adults who are also important friends and mentors. What if your kids go to them before they come to you, or in addition? You must not be jealous; only be thankful if your child is turning to godly counselors. Consistently pray for those people who touch your child's life.

When my husband was called into ministry and God led our family to join an inner-city church, my kids and I literally left all our friends as a sacrifice on the altar of obedience to God. (I share more about this personal story in the final chapter of this book.) As a homeschooling family, our social lives were mainly established around our relationships with the folks at church. It was very difficult to leave those familiar connections of fellowship. I knew things would not be the same because life is busy. Truthfully, most friendships are dependent upon an element of convenience. When it is easy to get together, you do. When it is not, you don't. Like any mom, as our family transitioned, I was mostly concerned about my kids having friends.

My son David has not had a friend his age at our church since we began ministering there. While there are several girls his age, there are no boys. I cannot count the many nights David and I prayed together for God to send a family with a boy his age to our church. After five years, that prayer still has not been answered the way I want it to be. However, God has provided greatly, in ways far beyond what I could have asked or imagined. God has built relationships between my son and his siblings that go deep. As the middle one of my three, David has a special relationship with his older sister and with his younger brother. He has a true friend in each of them. During these years, God has developed in David a heart for ministry. With no boys his age around, David gravitated to his Sunday school teacher and the youth pastor, who both reached out to him. I know these special men pray for my son, and I pray for them! I am so thankful for the power of their godly influence on David week after week.

Authenticity, the characteristic of being genuine and sincere, is a rare attribute for middlers. As parents, we have had experiences of our own with kids who were not authentic—true and real. There will always be those people who are only friends through the good times. Jesus spoke of this kind of friend in the parable of the prodigal son. In the story, a young man asked for his inheritance early. When his father agreed and gave him the money, he headed for the nearest big city and became a big spender. He had lots of big friends until his money ran out. Then his friends ran out, too. They weren't real. They were along for the ride—there for the good times, the free drinks, and the thrill of the ride.

For middle schoolers, friendship is often so precarious that it rests on a good hair day and wearing the right outfit. As much as we encourage our kids to make and keep good friends, they are most likely going to choose some duds as well. It is important that you, as an authentic parent, maintain a balance, staying involved so that you know when to reign in and when to let go. Dr. Tim Kimmel, in his book, *Why Christian Kids Rebel*, encourages parents to allow their children to make some mistakes when it comes to friends. "They might choose a bad influence or two and make some dumb choices," he says. "Let them feel the full force of the consequences of these choices, and don't rescue them from the messes they get themselves into. They will quickly learn invaluable principles about healthy relationships."[33]

It is difficult to watch these scenes play out in your child's life. Often, as a parent, I can see trouble coming. If I am not careful, however, I run the risk of pushing my child right into the very relationship I am hoping he will avoid! It is critical to your child's well-being that you step up your prayers for him and his friend, love on that friend, and get to know the friend's parents. You may certainly draw boundaries, but be careful that those boundaries don't become an invitation to temptation. Pray for balance!

In the case with my daughter and Mandy, their different perspectives on life became more and more evident. Eventually, Mandy moved away to live with her dad full time. Angry with God, she chooses to spend her teen years in rebellion against the Lord and her faith. Although they don't live in the same city any longer, Danya has kept in touch with Mandy, and she has never stopped praying for her. She understands that she has a responsibility to be an authentic friend to her. Recently, Mandy came in to visit her mom, and she asked if she could spend the night at our house. Well, things are different now. The ball is in our court! No longer an impressionable eleven-year-old, now Danya is an impressive sixteen-year-old. She knows who she is in Christ, and she knows what His Word says. So Mandy came over, and the two of them stayed up nearly all night talking. I went to bed, confident that if anyone was going to be influenced, it would be Mandy! And praise God, Danya shared Jesus with her! While Mandy hasn't completely surrendered to the Lordship of Christ, she was ready to listen that night. She respects Danya, and she knows that Danya has shown her authentic friendship.

Girls: Cat Fights and Cliques

For girls, relationships begin as mere acquaintances but transition into trusted bonds when they share their fears, disappointments, and victories with one another. Opportunities for a unique transparency develop, allowing them to shed their carefully composed images and just be themselves. This places an unusual vulnerability and a consequent responsibility on each side of the relationship.

When I was in middle school, I had a terrible crush on a boy who barely knew I was alive. My best friend was the only one I dared tell, and I trusted her with my every hope and dream for the one-sided romance. When we saw him one day in the library, she walked up to him and, giggling hysterically, told him that I liked him. I can still feel the hot blush that rushed to my cheeks as I wished for the tiled floor to become a sinkhole and swallow me alive. Today, secrets go global at the click of a camera phone, a forwarded e-mail, or a bulletin sent to hundreds of kids at once. What pressure! What stress! And girls—oh, dear!—our girls make foolhardy decisions at the insistence of revenge, retaliation, and one-upmanship, only to live with great regret over the turmoil they caused. What is up with that? Why do we females have such a problem with this?

They don't call them "catfights" for no reason, you know. I remember one night when Danya crept into my room and gently roused me from a deep sleep. "Mom," she whispered, "do you hear that?"

The howling cries of a rip-roaring cat fight jolted me into wakefulness. They sounded surprisingly like human voices, much like women shrieking. Several cats had converged on our porch for the second time that week to scream, spit, and hiss at each other, backs arched and tails quivering. Danya and I tapped on the window hoping to scare the cats off. Finally, I opened the front door and loudly shooed them away with the help of a broom.

The next morning I called a local vet, seeking a humane way to get rid of these cats. He advised me to do three things: Keep the porch light on, since cats prefer to fight under cover of darkness. Set out open containers of bleach, as cats do not like the odor, and cover the floor of the porch with plastic sheets because cats do not like slick surfaces.

Cat fights are an annual rite of spring. The breeding season stirs up territorial angst among felines as they guard their turf and compete for mating partners. *Catfights*, on the other hand, is a slang term referring to a physical or verbal altercation between two females. For girls, these are typical growing pains, a traditional rite of passage. Interestingly, we moms can effectively extinguish catfights and douse the power of cliques by using the same methods the vet suggested: Shed light on the situation, keep the disinfectant handy, and keep things slippery, so as not to allow the enemy to gain a foothold.

Keep the porch light on. Open communication is key when it comes to raising daughters. In order to know what is going on within their circle of friends, a mom must be intentional about getting in her daughter's loop. Try these ideas.

Dates. My mom and I had a regular date every Thursday. We went to my piano lesson, which provided twenty minutes of drive time for a chat. Afterwards, we would grab a burger and then go to the grocery store together. If something was going on with one of my friendships, we talked about it.

Listen. Listening is the most underestimated part of communication. Listen to your daughter when she wants to talk, even if it is not the best time for you. Do not interrupt! Give her your undivided attention. Try to listen without thinking about what you want to say next. A mother of teens once told me that when her daughter brought friends home on the weekends, they headed for the kitchen just as she was ready to go to bed. She said, "I know they've got the munchies, and they're ready to talk for a while, so I do whatever it takes to stay awake. I bake a pan of brownies and put on a pot of coffee. You can't schedule those times, but you should always be prepared for them."

Share. It is important for every girl to know that good friendships take time. Catfights and cliques are universal. Pull out your old memories and share the girl you were with the girl you are trying to raise.

Keep the disinfectant handy. Growing up and learning how to relate to other women is not easy. It is natural to be critical rather than caring and fault-finding rather than forgiving. These tendencies must be transformed through the cleansing power of God's Word. Write the following verses on note cards, and together, commit them to memory with your daughter.

"Love your enemies and pray for those who persecute you" (Matthew 5:44, NIV). With your guidance, your daughter can learn to pray for her enemies. Praying for one who is hurtful can not only release a spirit of forgiveness within the one who prays, but it can also open the door to a supernatural understanding of the offender. Praying together will lay the groundwork for approaching your daughter's teen years as prayer partners.

"Do not let any unwholesome talk come out of your mouths, but only what is helpful for building others up according to their needs, that it may benefit those who listen" (Ephesians 4:29, NIV). Gossip, teasing, name-calling, and sarcasm are standard fare for middler conversation, whether it is up close and personal or via e-mail and blog sites. Your daughter can go against the flow by remembering this verse and using her speech to encourage her peers with loving words that are kind and helpful.

"Don't show favoritism" (James 2:1, NIV). Help your daughter avoid the trap of superficiality. Lead her to understand that friends should not be chosen based on how they dress or how attractive they are. She will miss out on some great friendships by making judgments based on first impressions.

Keep it slippery. It is all too easy to remember the catfights you experienced as a girl and lose the perspective you have gained as an adult. Keep things slick by keeping in mind these squabbles are temporary. If you give them more weight than they deserve, these personality clashes can develop into miserable feuds that will last all the way through your daughter's high school years. You can have a great impact in three ways.

Parental involvement. When moms have an open network that seeks everyone's participation, girls often follow suit. If a girl is bullying or being bullied, on-line or in person, strong parental involvement can be essential for changing things.

Parental perspective. The "in" and "out" of the crowd is a revolving door. What seems like life or death drama today will often be forgotten by next week.

Parental influence. A Christian mom's influence can reach far beyond her family. Open your home to your daughter's friends, and encourage her to be a peacemaker when catfights occur.

The book of James invites us to confess our sins to one another.[34] It's easy for a teen to believe she is the only one who struggles with anger, laziness, or jealousy—or with pimples, oily hair, and self-esteem. After all, other girls make it look so easy! Life is much easier to manage with a trusted friend. Friendship itself is an extension of gratitude for what Christ has done. These powerful relationships prompt us to determine what other people need and provide it for them, with little thought as to what it might cost us.

If we can point our girls to the truth of God's love for them, they will be transformed into a channel of His love. It will be natural for them to share His love with others, even those who are unkind and hurtful toward them. Christ's love conquered death. It can conquer catfights and cliques, too.

Boys: Follow the Leader

Boys face their own unique set of challenges with friendships as they make their way through these years. My friend Mike[35] shared with me the story of a time when he realized, at fourteen, the dangers of following the crowd.

It was the annual youth trip to the falls, and Mike's dad had warned him, "Don't you jump off the falls like those kids did last year! They could've gotten killed!" The year before, there were some kids who jumped off the ninety-feet-high falls. It had seemed pretty cool when they returned talking about it. But the youth minister didn't think it was very cool. This year, he also issued stern warnings as the youth piled on the church van with their Bibles and duffle bags. There was to be no jumping off the falls.

But then two of Mike's friends returned from a secret jump and urged him to join them. "We've already done it once, and it was a blast!" they exclaimed, eager to include him. Although there was hesitation in his heart, it didn't keep him from following them. What Mike didn't realize was that someone was following him, too! Young Tyra was desperate to be a part of the crowd. She followed Mike and jumped the falls right behind him. As Mike remembers, once he realized someone was behind him and he saw Tyra, everything happened fast! She was hurt—badly hurt—screaming and crying out that there was something wrong with her legs. Waiting on the paramedics to come for Tyra, the subtle hesitation Mike ignored came back screaming lectures as he berated himself for his foolishness. He had seen the falls and knew they were dangerous. He had heard the warnings of his father and his youth pastor, yet it could not override the importance of keeping up with his friends.[36]

Our boys can get in a lot of trouble trying to keep up with their friends. Guys are naturally competitive. As a matter of fact, they were hard-wired by God for risk and adventure. Our job as moms is to help them keep that drive in perspective, not expressing it in thrill-seeking and circus stunts. In truth, God made boys with a sense of boldness and adventure in order to further His kingdom! They are the ones who have the innate capability to take the Gospel to the most desolate places. They are the ones equipped with a courageous sense of justice and loyalty that will give up everything for a cause they desperately believe in. It is crucial that we pray for God to channel the daring boldness of our young men into a passionate zeal for Christ.

Help your son understand that it takes real nerve to go against the crowd. It is a real risk to give up your life to a God you can't see. It takes a daring heart to live as the disciples did—at the feet of Jesus, ready to take off at a moment's notice. It takes a real man to put his faith and trust in the one and only Jesus Christ. And it is a real friend who will stand his ground in order to lead others—even just one—to salvation in God's Son. Pray daily for your son to be filled with the Holy Spirit and empowered by boldness to be an unashamed follower of God and influential leader of men.

Have you noticed that many times, our grown-up friendships are reduced to seventh-grade trivialities? Gossip, jealousy, and even snobbery exist easily among us "big girls," robbing our peace and setting us up for defeat. And what about following the crowd? Are you guilty of taking up the latest fad just because everyone else is doing it? Our kids are watching us. We must be the examples they need us to be: loving and praying for our enemies, guarding our speech, and showing others the open arms of Jesus Christ. Ask for God's help in loving people and establishing real friendships that glorify Him.

Toolbox

RULES FOR PLAYING IT SAFE ONLINE

Get involved. The best tool for online safety is parental involvement. Just as you would insist on knowing the kids your child brings home, insist on knowing the kids who are coming into your home via the Internet. Many parents set up their own MySpace or Facebook so they can be an online presence and get to know their kids' friends.

Draw the lines. Many parents will only allow their children to chat and message online with people they know personally. Most social networking sites are set up to allow parents to establish boundaries like these. Establish certain hours for being online, remembering homework and chores must be completed first.

Wise up. Learn how to check your computer's history to know what sites your child visits. If your middler is spending inordinate amounts of time online, find out where she is going and what she is doing.

Password protected. Know your child's password. Assure

your child that you will respect his privacy unless he gives you a reason not to.

Lights out. Just as you give a child a curfew, do not allow him to surf the Net late into the evening or after you have gone to bed.

Open-door policy. All the experts agree: Keep your computer in an open area that prohibits private viewing.

Zero tolerance. Don't allow your child to become an Internet gossip. Help him to keep his comments kind or keep his comments to himself.

Follow through with consequences. If your child does not conform to the boundaries you have in place, make the consequences swift and firm, and follow through.

SEVEN

BOYS AND GIRLS
ARE DIFFERENT

S tudies continue to reveal that the greatest influence on a child's attitude toward sex, and on his decision concerning how to use that gift, comes directly from his parents. Your kids want to know what you think. They want to be able to talk with you. They want you to be involved. I urge you to ground these middle school years on the virtue of chastity (purity). This will involve not a one-time conversation, but many discussions over the next several years.

Admittedly, talking about sexuality is not easy. However, as a mom, you need to be comfortable with it, especially when it comes to talking about these matters with your son. If you can't say "penis" with a straight face, go to your room, shut the door, and practice. Your son will know if you feel uncomfortable, and you can't leave all the sex discussions up to his dad! You will be missing out on a valuable part of parenting if you can't share your motherly advice and feminine perspective with him. I will never forget the advice given to me by a friend when I still had toddlers running around. She told a group of us young moms to make sure we were the first to talk to our kids about sex. In doing this, she said, you become the expert. Anything that anyone else says or does will forever be weighed against what Mom and Dad said first.

I met a precious mom at a conference where I spoke a few years ago. She was a single woman who was fostering several middle school-age girls. She was flipping through a copy of *Wise Up! Experience the Power of Proverbs,* which is my coming-of-age Bible study for girls, and she said, "You know, I really don't see any need for them to know about this stuff yet." As we talked, she explained that she wanted the girls in her care to be separated from the world. They lived on a country farm, and she did not allow television or the Internet in their home. She was proud of keeping the world at bay for these young girls.

I asked her, "Do you ever leave the farm?"

"Yes," she replied. "Once a week we come into town to do the shopping."

After a few more questions, I learned she did her shopping at the discount superstore. I had been to that store the day before, and I explained to her that the once-a-week trip into town was a trip into the world. This megastore had televisions suspended from the ceiling playing music videos that were not exactly wholesome. The blockbuster movie that year was a homosexual love story, and this store had huge displays of the DVD dominating the entryway. Tabloids spilled into every checkout lane, promoting the scandalous activities of immoral celebrities and politicians. And then there were people—from every walk of life, in every state of dress—frequenting this store. Here's the truth: While you may be hesitant to talk to your kids about sex, the world is not. And if I may be candid, the world does not have a sit-down, one-time talk about sex. The world's conversation about sex is ongoing, littered with misinformation and drenched in deception. Traps are set at every turn, targeting your teen, aiming for his downfall. What you think matters! Your child needs your wise input, your balanced perspective, and your prayerful counsel to make it through. And he needs it now.

Understanding the Pull of Pornography

When I was a young teen, I got my first job babysitting a six-year-old boy. He wanted to play hide and seek, so he ran to hide while I counted. His hiding place turned out to be the large, walk-in closet in his parents' bedroom. That is where I found him, crouching beside his dad's shoes, underneath a pornographic poster that was pinned to the wall.

Today, as a mother, I wonder what it was like for that little boy to grow up in a home thinking that pornography was normal. Since his daddy tacked pictures of naked women on the wall of his closet, he grew up thinking that all daddies—and therefore all men—did. I wonder how the little boy's mom could walk by that picture day after day as she went to get her own clothes out of the closet. Why didn't she rip it down? Unless her dad did the same thing, and she thought that was what all daddies did.

"Boys think pornography is harmless," says recording artist and Dove Award-winner Clay Crosse, author of the book, *I Surrender All: Rebuilding a Marriage Broken by Pornography*.

"It may feel naughty to them, and it may be something they wouldn't want others to know they are doing, but it won't feel like it's going to hurt them. They have to be convicted that it is wrong and it has damaging effects."[37]

Clay's first exposure to pornography was at a friend's house, when he was in the fourth grade. Although he had been raised in a Christian home, he didn't realize the long-lasting consequences the sin of pornography would have on his life, so he did not run away from the temptation. He did not call his parents to come and pick him up. He did not say, "No, thanks." He did not think, twenty years later, he would still struggle with a porn addiction he kept hidden from his wife, his family, and his thousands of fans. While we are quick to teach our kids the damaging consequences of drugs and alcohol, how do we guard our sons from the equally destructive effects of pornography, especially in a culture where sensuality is worshiped, women are exploited, and all forms of sexual expression are embraced?

The Christian home sets the standard for our children. Our actions and attitudes as moms and dads provide a living example that speaks louder to our sons than any lecture we might give. But are we missing the mark when it comes to making holiness a reality in our homes? Clay and his wife, Renee, believe many Christians, including themselves, have been guilty of neglect when it comes to setting a standard of righteousness.

By all outward appearances, the Crosses had the ideal Christian home. Yet they were very lax in the kinds of entertainment they chose through television, movies, and risqué comedy routines on HBO. "People can easily turn off what they know they need to be about when they are watching entertainment," Clay admits. "With no standard in my home, it actually made it easier for me to be watching pornography on the side because Renee and I were watching trashy stuff together and with our friends."

For us moms to come to an understanding of our sons, we have to realize their weakness when it comes to this battle and our responsibility to guard their hearts by helping them guard their eyes. The male species is wired for sight. The things you may not consider sensual, a growing boy with escalating hormones might find especially provocative. For a young man who has his sights set on godliness, this can be a huge hurdle in his life. He does not know how to handle it when this starts to happen to him. And he has choices to make. He can be like everybody else, or with your help, he can establish a standard of personal holiness.

- Keep lingerie magazines, including sales fliers from the local department store, out of sight. Just the other day, I opened a home-decorating magazine I subscribe to, and on the inside front cover was a nude woman advertising a moisturizing soap. I tore off the cover and threw it away. My sons don't pick up my decorating magazines, but I want to create a safe environment for them. That stuff goes out of my house.

- Filter what you are watching. Turn off the shows featuring scantily clad women and steamy love scenes. So what if it's not doing anything to you? Believe me, it is affecting your son! Also, take a closer look at teen shows on "kid-friendly" channels. Many young actresses are dressed to draw attention to every curve.

- Avoid the temptation of the Internet and cable by keeping computers and TV's out of your son's bedroom. No filter can do it all, and the problem is not whether or not you have a filter. Porn is a heart problem, and a filter will not fix that.

- Know how to check your Internet-surfing history. As a parent, you need to know where your kids go. You need to know whether or not they are using their Holy Spirit filter.

- Help your son make wise viewing decisions concerning movies, video games, and comic books.

"Pornography takes over a young man's life gradually," Clay shares. "One thing leads to another." Clay and Renee have established the ministry HolyHomes because they believe God has called Christian homes to be different. "We just want to encourage Christian homes out there to say, *No more!* No more in my house. I love my kids too much. I love my wife too much. And ultimately, I love the Lord too much to sit here on this life He's given me and not be focused on Him."

Worst Case Scenario: What If?

For Sylvia,[38] a mother of five, it was a playmate who introduced her fifth-grade son to Internet pornography. "We wouldn't have even known it if we hadn't been monitoring the computer," she says. "I was totally unprepared for anything like this, and frankly, I was angry."

While anger may be your first impulse, Clay has a word of caution for moms. "I think the worst thing is if Mom runs through the house, holding the magazine and saying, *What in the world are you doing? I can't believe this!* That can be a very damaging thing your son may never forget." Clay recommends that mothers stay calm and simply allow their husbands to step in. Because he understands much better what his son is going through, a father can relate in a real way. "But don't condemn," Clay says firmly. He believes it is best if a father has prepared his son through childhood. "Before they even start to feel those urges, even at seven or eight years old, talk to them about temptation," says Clay, "and how to deal with it."

Toolbox

THINKING ON THINGS ABOVE

The nature of sin. Establish with your son the common ground of sin we all share. Remind him that Christ came to save us from sin. We have hope because of His redeeming grace.

The normal of sin. Let him know he is normal. These thoughts do not make him a freak. He is just like every man, which, again, is why he needs Jesus.

The choice to sin. Agree to hold him accountable for his entertainment choices. He has a choice to avert his eyes, to turn the channel, and to refuse to see movies that have earned a bad review. (Check out movie reviews at Christian Web sites online.)

The victory over sin. Teach him to resist temptation the way Jesus did, through prayer and Bible study. Using Philippians 4:8 as a guide, help your son practice replacing fleshly thoughts with godly thoughts of things above. Let him know you are praying for him, and have a regular time each day to pray together.

"Christian thought is, first of all, redeemed thought," explains Jay Younts, author of *Everyday Talk: Talking Freely and Naturally about God with Your Children*.[39] "The goal for Christian thought is expressed in Psalm 19:14: May the words of my mouth and the meditation of my heart be acceptable to You, Lord, my Rock and my Redeemer."

When our children are ultimately concerned with whether or not their thoughts are acceptable to God, therein lies the payoff for Christian parents:

Kids who know that God is watching them even when no one else is looking.

Kids who feel it when their hearts are pricked by sin and weighted down by their need for forgiveness.

Kids who sense God's power and marvel at His overwhelming presence in their lives.

"One important goal of parenting is to teach your children to think God's thoughts after Him," reminds Younts. "Each day provides fresh opportunities to challenge your children to begin to embrace biblical, Christian thought as their own."

Single moms need to ask God to provide a Christian man who can serve as an accountability partner to their sons. Look for a coach, youth pastor, uncle, or grandfather who is willing to share in a real way with your son. It is important that boys understand every man struggles with the issue of pornography and that there is a God who is bigger than any temptation they face. His Word, His Holy Spirit, and His people can work together to provide the tools guys need to be overcomers.

Understanding the Pull of Pretty

My daughter and I went to hear the popular Christian abstinence speaker, Marilyn Morris, a few years ago. Marilyn was speaking to parents about many issues related to purity, and then she segued into a challenging talk on modesty. She said there are three reasons why a girl chooses to dress immodestly.

She's uninformed. It's possible no one has taken the time to educate her about what goes on in a young man's mind when he sees a girl dressed immodestly.

She's a tease. Some girls are fully aware of what they are doing. They enjoy the power trip they get from teasing the boys around them. This is cruel, manipulative, and sinful.

She's easy. Some girls dress immodestly because they are inviting boys to think of them as available for a sexual relationship. They are advertising with their appearance that they are up for grabs.

How is a young man supposed to know which of these

categories a girl falls into? According to Marilyn, a typical guy will put a girl in the category that best suits his desires. This is exactly how many girls have found themselves in dangerous situations. Girls need to understand that the way they dress makes a strong statement to the opposite sex about who they are, and it can quickly brand their reputation.

It was at this point that a thirty-something woman in the audience raised her hand. She was wearing a thin, wispy sundress with a scooping neckline. When Marilyn acknowledged her, she stood up and began to debate the modesty issue. "What if none of those reasons are true?" she asked belligerently. "What if you dress that way because it makes you feel pretty?"

Calmly, Marilyn explained that she believed if it made a woman feel pretty to flaunt her body, then it must be that she was uninformed (category one) and that no one had ever explained to her how her clothing choices were affecting the men around her. It would mean the woman was putting her need to feel pretty over her responsibility to not encourage another to sin.

The pull of prettiness, veiled in sensuality, still held a lure for this mom. I think it does for many moms, and that is why so many of our young girls dress immodestly. Assuming that your daughter does not fall into the latter two categories, by the time she is in middle school, you need to have a talk about modesty.[40]

Your daughter knows that boys and girls are different. Outwardly, of course, it's obvious. But she needs to understand that she is wired differently. A girl can look at a handsome young man and simply admire him. She thinks he's cute, and she might desire his attention. For the most part, her thoughts don't wander too far from that. Because females are emotionally wired beings, a girl craves relationship. She will imagine that cute young man talking to her and telling her things he would never share with anyone else: his hopes, his dreams, his goals, and how she fits into those plans like no one else ever could.

But guys are different. They are physically wired beings, visually stimulated. So if a girl is dressed in a skin-revealing tank top and short shorts, she has created a picture that a guy's mind is going to hang on to—whether he is thirteen or eighty-five! Because males are visual, they do not sit around wondering what a girl's hopes and dreams are. In fact, once a girl presents her body immodestly dressed, the guys have stopped thinking about her as a person. They are thinking about the body she has presented.

A young man's thoughts are at risk for reeling into lust almost before he can realize it. It is important for moms to understand that even when they think their daughters look cute, stylishly dressed in the latest fashions, the young men around them are not thinking cute thoughts. Their thoughts would make you very uncomfortable. Their thoughts would make you cringe. If a young man is a Christian, pursuing holiness, his desire is to gain control over those thoughts, but if he is not a Christian, those thoughts will have control over him. Be sure your daughter knows what not to wear.

Toolbox

WHAT NOT TO WEAR

What is immodest dress? Here is the dress code at my house, for both Danya and me.

We don't wear:

- Shoulder-baring dresses and tops
- Navel-baring tops
- Shirts that dip down and expose cleavage or the place where the breasts begin to curve
- Too-tight clothes
- Too-short shorts

Be sure your daughter has a full-length mirror in her room. Teach her to check out what she is wearing from all angles. Help her understand that she is serving her Christian brothers and, ultimately, serving the Lord by dressing modestly.

EIGHT

DRASTICALLY DIFFERENT DATING

n 1997, Joshua Harris, then twenty-one years old, wrote a groundbreaking book that would forever divide Christian singles and revolutionize the way the church views dating. The book *I Kissed Dating Goodbye* became a cultural phenomenon when young Harris dared to challenge Christians with a new perspective on dating. In the book, he chronicled his personal journey from a self-proclaimed "recreational dater," pushing the limits of purity, to a guy who had a new attitude toward dating. He resolved to avoid dating because he did not believe it was God's best way of doing things. He chose to go against the grain of common thinking, openly challenging the culture. The great debate he ignited has been stirring the hearts and refining the focus of young singles everywhere ever since. He writes,

> When I stopped seeing girls as potential girlfriends
> and started treating them as sisters in Christ, I discov-

ered the richness of true friendship. When I stopped worrying about whom I was going to marry and began trusting God's timing, I uncovered the incredible potential of serving God as a single. And when I stopped flirting with temptation in one-on-one dating relationships and started pursuing righteousness, I uncovered the peace and power that come from purity. I kissed dating goodbye because I found out that God has something better in store![41]

If Christians are supposed to be different from the world, then why is dating one area where we are the same? Christian kids rush into the boyfriend-girlfriend stage as early as everyone else. They are just as eager to label what should be friendships with romantic undertones. Like their secular counterparts, Christian young people are quick to give their hearts away and allow their focus to be distracted by exclusive relationships. Sadly, many Christian teens tend to associate their self-worth with whether or not they have a boyfriend or girlfriend. It starts early—in middle school.

I worried all through middle school because I didn't have a boyfriend. I believed the lie that claimed in order to be good enough, I had to be accepted by the guys—so I bided my time, waiting for my figure to develop, the braces to come off, and the day I could trade my glasses for contact lenses. When everything on the outside fell into place, I started dating. Unfortunately, everything on the inside needed a makeover, too, but that was not where my focus was. Caught up in the romance and drama of the teen scene, I broke a few hearts and had my own broken several times. I, too, pushed what I perceived as the limits of purity, jeopardizing my Christian testimony and my relationship with the Lord, and clearing the way for Satan to take a foothold in hearts I had no business trifling with. When it comes to worldly dating, I know what I'm talking about. You probably know, too, but allow me to illustrate it this way:

> Imagine I was in an accident, and your middle school-aged daughter or son came to see me in the hospital. There are machines hooked up to my body with those weird plastic sacs dispensing medicine one drop at a time into my bloodstream. I am covered in bandages. Both legs are in casts. Both arms are in slings.
>
> "Rebecca!" your child exclaims. "What happened?"
>
> "Well," I explain, "I was speeding. I was really in a hurry to get where I was going, and I just ignored all the speed limits that were posted and all the warning signs because I had somewhere I wanted to be."
>
> "Was anyone else hurt?"
>
> "Unfortunately, yes," I answer quietly. "I was having so much fun speeding along that I really didn't stop to think I might hurt someone else."
>
> "Is everyone going to be okay?"
>
> There is a long pause before I answer. "Everyone is going to be okay, but no one will ever be the same. Please, please," I beg your child, "don't speed!"[42]

De-emphasize Dating

I think dating is like speeding. It rushes the growing-up process, cheating our kids out of a safe, enjoyable journey. It sets up an opportunity for accidents that affect them and others. It often leaves our daughters and sons bruised and broken, and truthfully, no one is ever the same. Although "going out" is a popular phrase among middlers, and while everything about our culture encourages the dating scene, what we have chosen to do in our home is to de-emphasize dating.

Let me explain exactly what I am talking about when I use the word *dating*. I have crafted my own definition in order to be as specific as possible.

> dating—pursuing a romantic relationship with a member of the opposite sex for the purpose of being physically affectionate, having fun, and getting to know the other person. Marriage is not an immediate option because neither party is of marriageable age. Pursuit of said relationship is halted when either party's romantic feelings fade away or disappear completely. Dating resumes when romantic feelings are next discovered.

Kissing dating goodbye is, indeed, as bizarre as it sounds. After all, dating is a rite of passage revered by our American culture. It is a highlight of the growing-up years. *When will I be allowed to date?* is a question our kids ask at increasingly early ages! Often we parents are the very ones who rush the process, the very culprits who nudge our children into believing that dating is essential to a person's completeness. When Emilie's[43] parents divorced, her newly single mom quickly entered the dating scene. Five-year-old Emilie watched her mom's suitors arrive only to disappear, as one after another led to heartbreak. She observed that her mom's emotional highs and lows directly correlated with how a man was treating her. Emilie learned from her mother's behavior that men were essential to happiness as well as being the key component for drama. No wonder by the time she was in the sixth grade, Emilie was "going out." And her mother was quite pleased—encouraging the relationship by dropping Emilie and her "boyfriend" off at the movies and the mall. Did Emilie's mom realize she was jeopardizing her daughter's sexual purity, as well as her emotional well being, by encouraging dating at such an early age?

Josh McDowell, a noted Christian author and culture expert, conducted a study and found the age at which dating begins is strongly connected with sexual purity.[44] In the study, ninety-one percent of kids who began dating at the age of twelve had sex before high school graduation. In contrast, of the teens in the study who waited until the age of sixteen to date, only twenty percent had sex before they graduated.

When you ask your second grader who her boyfriend is, or when you want to know who your nine-year-old son is "sweet on," you are instilling premature thoughts and pushing innocence aside. You are setting your kid up. When you offer to host the first boy-girl party for your middler, and then you disappear into another part of the house for its duration, you are setting your kid up. When you tease your child about an innocent friendship being the groundwork for a romance, you are setting your kid up. Get a hold of yourself!

What if we set our kids up for something else? What if

we prepared them to look at dating from a new perspective? What if we actually empowered them with the opportunity to look at this cultural tradition from a completely different vantage point? What about not dating?

Not Dating?

Most teens are incredulous when you suggest the idea of not dating. Some ask, "If I don't date, how can I be prepared for marriage?" Others say dating is essential because, "Without dating, how will I know who God has for me? God is not just going to drop the right person in front of me." Parents, too, accept dating as a fact of life. I completely understand those views. After all, admittedly, I dated. But I want to offer you a couple of new ideas in response. First, did you ever stop to think that going through the dating-breaking up-dating cycle is not preparation for marriage, but for divorce? In *I Kissed Dating Goodbye,* Joshua Harris explains.

> We see so much divorce and betrayal in our society today. Take a quick count—how many of your friends come from broken homes? I believe that this trend will only increase as each generation begins to practice short-term love in dating relationships earlier and earlier. It seems that dating as we have come to know it doesn't really prepare us for marriage; instead it can be a training ground for divorce. We cannot practice lifelong commitment in a series of short-term relationships ... Who wants to marry someone who will ditch a relationship the moment romantic feelings wane? Who wants to marry a per-

son who has developed a habit of breaking up and finding someone new when the going gets tough?

We need to realize that the lifelong commitment so many of us desire in our future marriages cannot be practiced or prepared for in a lifestyle of short-term relationships.

Second, much of the confusion Christian parents and teens experience when it comes to dating exists because this modern-day tradition is not mentioned in the Bible. God's Word was written in a time, at a place, and to a people familiar with betrothal. Arranged marriages and even legal customs were firmly in place to provide for a man and a woman to be linked together to raise a family and to continue a lineage.

Protecting Purity

Interestingly, when a couple's love story is mentioned in the Bible, the record shows that God actually did drop the right woman in front of the man who was looking for her. For example, who can forget the story of Adam and Eve? While Adam was sleeping, God formed Eve from one of his ribs, and then He brought her to him.[45] In another love story, Father Abraham actually sent his trusted servant in search of a wife for his son, Isaac. Through prayer, completely relying on God, the servant was able to spot Rebekah immediately, and she agreed to be Isaac's wife, though they had never met![46] And then there is my favorite Old Testament couple, Ruth and Boaz. Ruth was a beautiful young widow, and the Bible suggests that Boaz was quite a bit older than she. Upon her arrival in Bethlehem, she "just happened" to go to work in

Boaz's field. When Ruth let him know that she was willing to be his wife, he said, "God bless you, my dear daughter! What a splendid expression of love! And when you could have had your pick of any of the young men around" (Ruth 3:10, Msg). When we de-emphasize dating, we are helping our child display a splendid expression of love to his future spouse. The choice to forego dating (as our culture knows it) guards the heart, in order that it may be given fully to the future spouse, with no outstanding emotional ties. It gives kids the chance for real-time relationships, by providing the opportunity to develop lifelong friendships with persons of the opposite sex.

Why waste kisses? Why squander intimacy? Why grieve the Holy Spirit by defiling the body—the temple of God? Wouldn't it be better if our kids could look back on their teen relationships without regrets but with plenty of fun memories?

I must admit that I have been brainwashing my children against dating since they were very young. At times, I think there is really very little any parent can do when it comes to this sort of thing, but then again, that is what the enemy would have me believe—he would have me believe that I have no influence on my child, that my relationship with my child will end as these years approach, and that I can do very little about it. But no! That is simply not true. One of the ways I have de-emphasized dating is in drawing a picture for my kids, when they were little, of what their teenage years would look like. I didn't talk about dating and driving as the most important part of those years. Instead, I described how they could do anything, explaining, "When you're a teenager, you'll be old enough to really explore different careers and life skills and see in what direction God has you aimed." I would speak ruefully about my teen days spent mostly on the phone or watching television. Oh, what wasted time! But then, smiling, I would add, "But look what you can do! You'll have time to pursue the desires of your heart!"

Several years ago, just as I was beginning to talk to my daughter about what it would be like to be a teenager, there was a story in the news. Anu Kotha, a fourteen-year-old high school freshman in Florida, studied Resveratrol, a compound found in grapes and believed to be a powerful antioxidant, for her science project. Because cancer ran in her family, she wanted to see if she could be a part of the cure. This young teen went to the Moffit Cancer Center in Tampa and asked the researchers if she could work in their labs and put Resveratrol to the test. Impressed with her data as well as her determination, they agreed. The result? Anu discovered the compound could kill tumor cells while having no effect on the healthy cells.[47]

At fourteen, Anu was using her time to learn and pursue research, which she already knew she loved. She was on a mission to find a cure for cancer. And no one was telling her she couldn't do it. I remember taking that article and showing it to my daughter, just delighting over this teenager who was doing something besides pursuing a social life! Over and over I would tell my kids, "What do you want to do when you're a teenager? Daddy and I will be paying your bills. You don't have to worry about a family or a roof over your head. You can do whatever you want to do, and we will help you." The catch here is that you have to mean it.

There is a war being waged on your middler's purity.

You've got to join her in her fight to stay pure! If you choose to discourage dating (as per my definition), then you can encourage a host of other great things: entrepreneurship, volunteerism, and excellence in academics, sports, and the arts. You can also encourage her to embrace a radical mindset that demands more from life than to simply do "what everyone else is doing."

My family attended a wedding a few years ago where the bride and groom had chosen drastically different dating. Sara and Troy had never kissed each other. They had chosen a higher standard for their dating: purity. The year they spent getting to know each other and each other's family was also spent diligently guarding each other's purity, which started by keeping their kisses for after they were married. We had a front row seat for their first kiss! It was the most exciting wedding I have ever been to, and today, they are a beautiful Christian couple—in sync with God and with each other.

Drastically different dating encourages your child to interact with the opposite sex as friends—brothers and sisters in Christ—each wanting the higher good, the better part, the bigger piece, for the other. Encourage your child to begin praying now for his future spouse, asking God to guard her purity until the day He brings them together.

Toolbox

DRASTICALLY DIFFERENT DATING (DDD) DEFINED

Includes. DDD involves group settings. Everyone is

included, even younger siblings! DDD looks like a bunch of friends getting together to have some fun—because that's what it is! Normally, a dating relationship becomes exclusive as two people get wrapped up in each other physically, mentality, and emotionally. DDD doesn't sacrifice time with friends and family.

Encourages. DDD means celebrating the good things that happen: a good grade, a new sibling, a winning game, or a successful performance. Friends don't really need a special occasion to get together, but if someone could be encouraged by a bit of a party atmosphere, then do it!

Invites. Where do you stand when your kids want to have people over, Mom? This is often one of the hardest things for us to do as parents! Allow God to stretch you if you are not comfortable when it comes to opening your home. Believe me—you want your kids and their friends at your house! You want them to feel comfortable there, and you want it to be first choice. You can make it happen.

Ministers. Besides going to the movies and the mall, encourage your kids to get together with others for service projects. This really doesn't look like traditional dating! It means finding somewhere to volunteer, to intern, and to serve.

Protects. DDD does not play games with people's hearts. It protects hearts. It waits and it prays, and in so doing, your teen learns to really love others unselfishly—as Christ loves us.

NINE

INDEPENDENCE VERSUS REBELLION

t was a cold, snowy Sunday when my friend Chris first discovered our inner-city church. His own fellowship had opted out of holding services due to the inclement weather, so he began driving until he found a church that looked like it was open. What he saw when he entered our sanctuary that day surprised him: Worship was being led by our young teens. Two things impressed him. First, these teenagers were doing a great job. He loved how their energy and enthusiasm made up for their obvious lack of experience! Second, he was amazed to find a church family that would humble themselves to be led by their youth. Looking around, he noticed a mostly senior citizen audience. Their love and support for the kids, however, were visibly evident.

Time to Step Up Your Game

Our middle schoolers are ready to stretch their wings. It is up to us to provide those opportunities for them, making our love and support visibly evident. Perhaps one of the hardest things for us as parents of middlers is muddling through this transition ourselves. I once interviewed Robert Lewis, author of *Raising a Modern Day Knight* and pastor-at-large for Fellowship Bible Church in Little Rock, Arkansas, who shared with me that today's parents tend to move away from being directional parents to authoritarian parents, thinking that if they can control all the factors, it will protect their children. "What I've learned over the years," he said, "is that parents who become authoritarian, who set a lot of rules, who are constantly suspicious, and who have a lot of punishments for things, do more damage than good."[48] In other words, many times during this season, we tend to tighten the reigns, rather than cutting our kids some slack. It is because we are afraid. We fear for our children's safety, health, and well-being. Where there is the presence of fear, there is the absence of faith. This approach to parenting will not serve us well.

I think many moms can identify with being a control freak! This controlling spirit is rooted in fear, which comes from a lack of faith. I will be the first to admit I have a hard time letting go, but I must learn to trust God with my kids. After all, they are much better off in His hands than in mine. Even as I write this, my two older kids are preparing to go with our youth group for several days of winter camp. My worrier gets turned on as I think about who will be driving, where the group will be staying, what they will be learning, and who will be leading. I have all kinds of questions and concerns! I often look back on my own teen years and wonder how my parents did it. How did they let go? I don't recall my mother showing any reluctance about my going on youth trips. I don't recall her asking a hundred times about who was going or drilling my youth pastor about his driving record. No, Mom was always cheerful and excited for me, and if there was any hesitation on her part, I certainly did not know about it. I loved those trips because they gave me a sense of independence. I was in charge of myself, although under the watchful supervision of other adults.

Timm Glover, a Licensed Clinical Pastoral Therapist (LCPT) at Middle Tennessee Medical Center, acknowledges that this is classic early adolescent behavior.[49]

> "Separation is beginning to occur. For your early adolescent, it is a sense of *becoming myself.* This is called individuation. It's a sense of who one is, independently of her parents. There are some typical characteristics of it that let parents know what is happening. Your child doesn't want you to kiss her in public. She doesn't want to be cuddled at home. But at the same time, she is yearning for that. You just have to negotiate it on her terms."

Glover says he always notices inner turmoil as kids are moving from dependency to independency, developing the self, learning to regulate the emotions, and coming to terms with an ever-changing body image. After all, when you think about it, this is a scary time for your child, too! She realizes that she is moving from being the one who is taken care of to being the one who is responsible for taking care of herself. It can also be an angry time, especially for our sons. When cravings for independence come along, they are accompanied by the stark realization that it is still a good distance away. "Some of the tendency toward anger or aggression is natural, because you've got the testosterone kicking in, so there is a hormonal element that comes with it," Glover explains. "Males are designed to be defenders, warriors, and protectors. There's a spiritual benefit to having that ability as it relates to the spiritual defense of the family. As Christian parents, we want to see that guided under the virtue of fortitude (courage)."

Certainly, independence can be a good thing! Children were created to be independent from their parents, but growing always in total dependence on God, growing away from the earthly and toward the heavenly.

Between the Manger and the Ministry

Have you ever stopped to think that Christ Himself was not exempt from the middle school years? Born a babe in a manger, He grew and endured the same "growing pains" we do. In fact, while the Scriptures are mostly quiet between that holy night of birth and thirty years later, when Christ's ministry began, God graciously gives us a glimpse of Jesus, the twelve-year-old boy.

> Every year His parents went to Jerusalem for the Feast of the Passover. When He was twelve years old, they went up to the Feast, according to the custom. After the Feast was over, while His parents were returning home, the boy Jesus stayed behind in Jerusalem, but they were unaware of it. Thinking He was in their company, they traveled on for a day. Then they began looking for Him among their relatives and

friends. When they did not find Him, they went back to Jerusalem to look for Him. After three days they found Him in the temple courts, sitting among the teachers, listening to them and asking them questions. Everyone who heard Him was amazed at His understanding and His answers. When His parents saw Him, they were astonished. His mother said to Him, "Son, why have You treated us like this? Your father and I have been anxiously searching for You."

"Why were you searching for Me?" He asked. "Didn't you know I had to be in My Father's house?" But they did not understand what He was saying to them. Then He went down to Nazareth with them and was obedient to them. But His mother treasured all these things in her heart. And Jesus grew in wisdom and stature, and in favor with God and men.

Luke 2:41–52, NIV

The writer of the Gospel of Luke tells this story of Jesus at the temple, specifically including the fact that Jesus was twelve years old. Jesus and His parents went to Jerusalem for the Passover festival. When the celebration was over, Mary and Joseph started home to Nazareth, but Jesus, unnoticed by them, stayed behind in Jerusalem. The two didn't miss Jesus at first, because they assumed He was with friends among the other travelers. But when He didn't show up that evening, they started to look for Him. Unable to find Him, they returned to Jerusalem to search for Him there. They found Him in the Temple, sitting among the religious teachers, discussing deep questions with them and startling them with His profound answers. What a picture that must have been!

Sincerely questioning His parents' concern, Jesus explained that they should have known He would be in His Father's house. And here's the part of the story that I love: He returned to Nazareth with them and was obedient to them. There at home, He continued growing. He asserted His independence, but He accepted His earthly parents' authority and submitted to them. He realized He still had more growing to do! That's the example our children need to go by.

Christ exemplified the virtue of meekness. Meekness can be defined as the quality of being mild, patient, and slow to anger. It means submitting to authority and yielding one's will. Please do not confuse this with weakness. Meekness is a virtue that, in order to be cultivated in everyday life, actually takes a great deal of strength. It includes the undervalued characteristic of teachability combined with self-control. True meekness occurs for you as an individual when you know you could push the envelope, but you choose to submit anyway. I think that's what we see Jesus doing here. He knew that He could have easily hung out all day with the teachers. He could have been their prodigy. But God gave Him parents to remind Him that it wasn't time. Even for the Christ, parents were in place to provide balance.

In our country, the teen years are characterized by rebellion against parents. Independence does not equal rebellion. These are two different things. Rebelling against Christian parents is ultimately rebelling against God, and your kids need to know that. Moms and dads often mistake the natural progression of independence as rebellion. How do you discern between the two? When independence morphs into the pride of life, manifesting itself in a child who disregards the Lordship of Christ, that's rebellion—and that's sin.

Our middlers long one day to be grown up and the next to be just kids. They are not quite ready for full-blown independence. But they are definitely ready to try new things. We want to encourage their budding independence within boundaries. If you don't offer them the time, the place, and the space to stand on their own two feet, they might just stage a revolution of their own! There are several areas where your child can cultivate his independence: with his own money, his own chores, and his own time.

Financial Freedom[50]

Is your child interested in starting his own business? Thanks to generous allowances, indulgent grandparents, and even us well-intentioned moms, many children simply are not motivated to pursue creative entrepreneurship because they already get everything they want. They do not need money, so unfortunately, they are being denied the opportunity to invest in themselves and work for the things they want. How can you promote a strong work ethic, creative business skills, and the opportunity for financial education in your own home? Encourage a sense of entrepreneurship in your kids.

For Ben and Sam Wilson, the idea of running their own business came about quite naturally. They were watching their dad, Todd "The Family Man" Wilson, support his ministry by selling resources at his speaking events and through his Web site. When Ben, then twelve, found a reasonably priced cap gun he really liked, he figured he could sell it to the hundreds of kids he saw trailing behind their parents at his dad's conferences. "If there was anything I did to pro-mote a sense of entrepreneurship, it was to instill in my kids that they could and should try any good idea that they have," says Todd, on-line at www.familymanweb.com. "The biggest killer of entrepreneurship is fear."

Let your children try, even if it means letting them fail. Remember, Thomas Edison made thousands of unsuccessful attempts before perfecting the light bulb!

In order to really encourage your child's independence, take a few steps back. Be careful to realize that your child's business should be just that—his own! "My wife and I helped our children place orders for their products, but that's about all we did," notes Todd. "They did the research, decided what they would sell, and set the price. We acted as consultants and encouragers, but we never pushed them." Todd admits there was a time when he tried to paint a grander picture and show the boys how they could take their business to the next level, but they were not ready to go there. Keep in mind that your child, who has no mortgage or insurance premiums to pay, may be satisfied to keep his business small.

At its best, work should reflect a person's passion. Find out what your child loves to do, and watch for potential busi-ness ideas. Jeremy White, a CPA and co-author of the book, *Your Kids Can Master Their Money*, recommends that parents move beyond the traditional one-time lemonade stands and branch into areas where their kids can actually earn money. In the book, he suggests a brainstorming session that includes not only traditional self-employment ideas, such as develop-ing a seasonal lawn-mowing venture or weekend babysitting business, but also brings in progressive, new prospects such as Web site design and retail. The Internet gives today's children the chance to bypass yesterday's yard sale and open their own global store through sites like eBay.com. With parental supervision, they can enjoy accepting bids on their used toys, books, and even collectibles such as Disney souvenirs and baseball cards.

Keep in mind, however, that your child may or may not be an entrepreneur. "You would never want to try to make a non-entrepreneur into an entrepreneur," cautions Todd. "Not only will you frustrate yourself, but you will also frustrate your child."

Toolbox

FINANCIAL PEACE BEGINS AT HOME

Opportunities. Look for money motivators the next time you hear the words, "I wish I had one of those!" Give your child the opportunity to earn extra money through extra household chores or remodeling projects around the house.

Dreams. Give her time to dream up creative ways of making money on her own. What does she like to do? Babysit? Clean house? Garden? Take care of pets? Sometimes a seasonal summer job is the best place to start, offering a service for neighbors who are vacationing.

Guidelines. Together you can establish spending guidelines that include pre-determined amounts for giving and saving. Always let your kids make their own decisions on how to spend the bulk of the money they earn. Personal experience will teach them the importance of being a thrifty shopper, the significance of saving for a rainy day, and the value of hard work.

Radical Responsibility

I stared at the trash can that was spilling over with garbage, and slowly exhaled. Then I called my kids into the kitchen. Nodding my head in the direction of the stuffed-to-overflowing trash receptacle, I asked, "What's wrong with that?"

"With what?" My youngest, a ten-year-old boy, shrugged his shoulders.

"What are you talking about, Mom?" For my thirteen-year-old son, whose brain cells are temporarily diverted by yet another growth spurt, standing in the kitchen has reminded him that he is hungry. He completely missed the trash problem once he spotted the fridge.

Their older sister sighed with an air of superiority. "She's talking about the trash, boys," she announced. "It's full, and no one has taken it out."

I then began to explain to the children the real problem. Instead of someone—anyone—seeing a full bin and taking care of it, all three had just continued to cram trash in. Each one was thinking that eventually someone else would come along and empty the trash can. The real problem was a heart attitude of laziness. It was a "not my job" mindset that could eventually spell disaster for our family, and even for my children's future families.

Your child wants to be independent; he wants more freedom—yet he can't seem to remember to put the toilet seat down or pick up his dirty socks from the floor. I believe it was Spiderman who said, "With great power comes great responsibility." Perhaps the reverse is true as well. Try giving your middler more responsibility, and he may see in that, he does have more power. Chores are a great place to start.

My friend Sandy has always taught her kids to do chores. From the time they were barely toddlers, she had them working with her, learning how to do all the necessary jobs around the house. Sandy knew she could do the work more quickly herself. She knew most of her kids' friends did not have to do chores. But she was always looking at the bigger picture, and she said simply, "I don't care to raise sloppy adults."

Author Patricia Sprinkle agrees, with one exception. "I never use the word 'chore,'" she notes. "I use the word 'skill.' Keeping a house is a skill. Preparing nutritious meals, doing the laundry—these are skills that children need to learn."[51] Sprinkle, author of *Children Who Do Too Little*, believes, "When moms do not teach their children these skills, they are crippling them for adulthood."

Teaching children how to take care of themselves and the home they will eventually live in should be every parent's goal. And according to Sprinkle, learning housework and home maintenance is critical knowledge for the business world as well. "They learn responsibility," she notes. "Doing these tasks teaches kids how to apply themselves to work they may not especially enjoy. It helps them understand that some jobs must be done whether you feel like it or not."

When it comes to chores, children's enthusiasm runs opposite to their ability. The less able they are to do something, the more eager they are to do it! You can capitalize on their willingness by keeping this in mind: Do not expect perfection. You are teaching your child. Whatever the task, you will be doing it again soon; such is the very nature of chores. Keep yourself from re-doing what your child has done. Sandy says, "If you go behind them and correct everything they do, what was the purpose in their doing it? No child wants to see his work re-done." Allow your child to value the joy of a task completed by his own hands, at his own level of ability.

Children who do too little have moms who do too much. They are not the only ones who will reap the benefits of a daily education in life skills. "Look at the results for your family at the far end," encourages Sprinkle. "Once your family is functioning as a team, you have more free time." Sandy can attest to this. After investing so much time training her children in life skills, today she has tweens and teens who can clean the house, prepare a meal, and do their own laundry. "It has definitely paid off," she says. "When my kids were small, I let them do things even though they didn't do it perfectly. Today they have grown into their chores, and they do as good a job as I do."

Another area ripe for teaching responsibility is with your child's schoolwork. Are you constantly prodding and pushing your child to complete her assignments? A friend of mine was frantically completing her daughter's science notebook the night before it was due. When I asked how it became her (the mom's) responsibility, she replied crossly, "Well, it's not! My daughter has known about this for weeks!"

"Then why are you doing it for her?" I asked.

"I don't want her to get in trouble!" she answered.

Getting in trouble is the expected outcome for neglecting a school assignment. Why would you want to cheat your child out of learning the natural order of events? Do you have all sorts of free time yourself? Are you the one accepting the grade? Of course not. Let your child experience the inherent bumps and bruises along the way to being a responsible adult.

As a homeschooling mom, my kids have always answered to me for their school assignments. Consequently, in helping them learn to be responsible, I have taken a "hands off" approach when it comes to the other teachers in their lives. For example, my daughter was held accountable to her piano teachers. I chose not to interfere in those relationships. When Mrs. Jeri or Mrs. Lisa assigned Danya lessons for the week, I did not stand over her to see that those pieces were completed. While I did help Danya establish a regular practice time each day, it was always up to her if she spent that time working on what her teacher had assigned or if she spent it just doing her own thing.

Then there are coaches. While I have witnessed mom after mom telling those precious volunteer coaches how to do their jobs, I have taken a backseat. I'll admit, my husband helps keep me in line in that department! But it didn't take me long to understand that what I was seeing at the games was a direct result of what happened at the practices. When one of my boys doesn't give his best effort in practice, the coach doesn't give him as much playing time. And that, I continue to understand, is between my son and his coach. Believe me, I don't want to trade places with either of them!

Toolbox ────────────────────────────

RESPONSIBILITY REMINDERS

Attitude counts. "Render service with a good attitude, as to the Lord and not to men, knowing that whatever good each one does, slave or free, he will receive this back from the Lord" (Ephesians 6:7–8, NIV).

No complaining allowed. "Do everything without grumbling and arguing" (Philippians 2:14, NIV).

Work glorifies God. "Therefore, whether you eat or drink, or whatever you do, do everything for God's glory" (1 Corinthians 10:31, NIV).

──────────────────────────────────────

Pass the Plate

I entered my middle school years during the Carter Administration. I don't remember much about the Carter presidency, but I do remember Amy, the president's daughter.

She was just about my age, and I felt sorry for her. I wrote about Amy Carter in my book, *Wise Up! Experience the Power of Proverbs.*

> Whenever I saw pictures of Amy in the newspaper, she wasn't smiling. She had long blond hair and thick, round glasses. She was neither glamorous nor fashionable; she was just an ordinary girl who was getting a lot of attention that she probably didn't want.

Everywhere she went, she was accompanied by Secret Service men. She was driven to school in a limousine. Cameras and reporters were always close by. It must have been difficult to be the President's daughter, especially at such an awkward time of growing up. Who wants the eyes of a nation watching when you're buying your first bra, or starting your period, or trying to figure out boys? Those are the days when a girl wants to be left alone.

Amy, however, managed to find a getaway. Her parents had a tree house built for her on the White House grounds. It was a quiet, personal retreat for a growing girl. It was a place where she could go and think, or pray, or just be still.

Kids need a place to be independent—to be alone and think. If your teen shares a room with a sibling, consider sanctioning times for each to enjoy some uninterrupted solitude. Think of how much you enjoy time alone: time to talk to God and time to listen to Him.

When I was a kid, it was our family tradition to go out to eat every Friday night. My mom was a teacher, and this was a special treat for her as well as everyone else. By the time I entered the seventh grade, however, things had changed. My sister had gone away to college, and since I had plenty of quality meals around the table with my folks (we ate breakfast and dinner together), I asked them if I could stay home on Friday nights while they went out. They agreed. I spent those evenings doing everything from trying new hairstyles to playing the piano and singing at the top of my lungs. With the house to myself, I would play the stereo as loud as it would go and dance around just being silly. There were quiet moments, as well, when I would sit down and talk out loud to God, enjoying real communion with Him, realizing anew His very presence and His plan for my life. It's from these memories, coupled with my own growing children, that God led me to develop my Bible studies for teens. I understood when it was time to move my children toward their individual, independent walks with the Lord, and I wanted to do everything I could to support that discipline in their lives.

It is absolutely crucial that we motivate our daughters and sons to study God's Word on a daily basis, not because they have to, but because they want to. If, as parents, we truly believe that Scripture is: God-breathed, useful for teaching, rebuking, correcting and training in righteousness, and able to equip us for every good work,[52] if we truly believe that it holds the key to every real success in life, then its study should be something that we give our lives to and that we lead our kids to give their lives to as well.

Think of it this way: We spoon feed our babies for a limited time. Eventually, as they start grabbing things off our plate, we teach them how to eat on their own. We get them their own plates, with smaller portions of the same things we're eating. We teach them how to chew! (Remember that? As a new mom, I had no idea that my baby wouldn't chew instinctively! I had to teach her everything, and she learned best by watching me.)

The same is true in mapping out your child's relationship with God. First, you spoon feed, diligently teaching him the Scriptures through exciting stories and short memory verses. Feed him also by allowing him to see you stealing away for a quiet moment in God's Word. Soon, you will realize that your child is now grabbing things from your spiritual plate and asking for more of what you've got! So get him a plate of his own: a new Bible, a study book, a concordance, and Bible software. Eventually, you will find that he is feeding himself. Lately, I'm finding a new day has come for my family; my teens are moving into new roles, often serving me spiritually as they share what they're learning in their relationships with God.

• • • • • • • • • •

TEN

MOTIVATING SPIRITUAL
DISCIPLINES

From the time we were in the sixth grade, my best
friend Angie and I spent most of our time together.
If we weren't in the same class, we would pass notes
in the hall. If she wasn't at my house, I was at hers. And when
we weren't together, of course, there were marathon phone
conversations. We told each other everything.

When Angie and I had disagreements, we hammered
them out. The "silent treatment" never lasted long. Both of
us enjoyed writing, so if there was something that we couldn't
talk about, we would write about it until it was settled
between us. Our friendship thrived because we stayed constantly connected.

In the middle of our sophomore year of high school,
Angie and her family moved two states away. The constant
contact was severed. The tie was loosed. It was a wretched
parting that deeply wounded our tender teenage hearts. At
school, I was wandering around trying to shake the uncom-

fortable feeling of loneliness when a friend came up and put her arm around me. "You look like a fish out of water without Angie," she said kindly. Indeed, that's how I felt.

A Constant Connection

In the weeks that followed, I gradually became aware of another Friend who had been trying to get my attention. This Friend desired a constant connection with me. Because Angie and I had been inseparable, I hadn't even noticed His still, small Voice, whispering His love and availability, reaching for me with the promise of a friendship that would never move away.

I was formed with a desperate, inborn need to know God and be known by Him. The enemy tries to satisfy this longing by placating my wicked flesh with a variety of pleasures intended to distract me. In the same way that a pacifier meets the need of a hungry baby, so my soul desires are fulfilled by the world: *temporarily*. As a girl, my best friend could not fill that need. As a woman, my husband cannot meet that need. Food, pleasure, success, recognition, prosperity—these cannot meet my heart's truest need for Jehovah's companionship.

I long to be mindful of His nearness twenty-four hours a day, but I continue to be easily distracted. In order to maintain my relationship with Him, I start with a morning quiet time, defined as time spent alone with God, intentionally seeking to build a stronger relationship with Him through prayer and Bible study. It is hard work to maintain the habit of this connection. Honestly, it goes against my human nature to get up instead of sleep, to concentrate on the Lord instead of my "to do" list, to be peaceful in His presence instead of fidgety at His feet. There have been times when I've given Him the silent treatment. Then I read something He has written, and I remember that He has already hammered out our differences on the cross. He has made the ultimate connection between God and man. Without Him, I am like a fish out of water.

If all that's true, then why has the greatest challenge of my Christian life been maintaining a daily quiet time? As a college student, I was devoted to this faith practice of time alone with God. I often stayed awake late to meet with God or enjoyed a leisurely morning time with Him. However, after I married and graduated, it seemed to be more difficult to find time to connect with the Lord. Job responsibilities made early rising mandatory, and it was tough to beat the clock in order to spend time with God.

After a long day, my husband and I spent evenings with friends or relaxed in front of the television. Night after night of good intentions fell sway to heavy-lidded alibis. Early morning alarms were set but repeatedly missed the mark, silenced with a press of the snooze button. And then children came along.

The realities of parenting not only increased my desire to meet with God every day, but I realized anew my critical need for His power and presence in my life. I often wondered, "How could He have entrusted me with the care of these hearts?" I felt so inadequate. I wanted to spend time with God. I longed to hear His voice through prayer and Bible study. But still, that did not make establishing a daily quiet time easy. As parents, we battle the enemy on several fronts when it comes to being consistent in our walks with God, and it is no wonder! It is on our knees where we learn to truly fight for the souls of our children. It is on our knees where God tells us the things we need to know as parents. After all, He wants to partner with us in this endeavor! And as our children walk into these middle school years, the enemy has his evil eye on them. He wants to take them out now, crushing the hope of these middle years and defeating them before they ever make it to high school.

The enemy is sneaky. In order to do battle, we must take full advantage of the power found in listening to God! Recently, I was growing concerned about my son Derek. He is my youngest, and he is the picture of his people-loving, ministry-oriented dad. The Lord has blessed Derek with a gift of joy that spills onto everyone he meets. But for a couple of weeks, the joy had gone missing. Instead, Derek had become argumentative and defensive. In praying for him one day, I asked the Lord what it was that had seemingly taken over my son's demeanor and attitude. As I waited before the Lord, He gave me one word. It was the name of a video game—a game I thought to be harmless. An Internet search led me to an article by a Christian dad who had enjoyed the very game my son was into, until he reached a certain level of the game and found it to be something very different from how the game began. It contained elements of the occult. This dad's article was frightening news to me. I knew I did not want that game in our home.

Although I strongly encourage parents to take an interest in the things their children are involved in, video games hold absolutely no appeal for me. I began to pray that when I confronted Derek, he would be honest with me. I knew I wasn't going to start playing the actual game in order to find out if the article was true. I also prayed that God would be working on Derek's heart, so that what I was going to ask of him would be met with a submissive spirit and not a defiant one.

Later that morning, I took Derek aside and simply told him I believed something was wrong. I shared with him what the Lord had told me. Immediately, Derek hung his head and replied, "Mom, I've been thinking about that this morning."

Prayer works! Only God could have spoken to both our hearts at the same time, leading us both to obedience. God pricked my heart to wake up as to what was going on in my home; God prepared Derek's heart to receive the admonishment from me and submit to what God wanted us to do about it.

Every day, I need time—even if it's just a few moments—to get away from the stresses of motherhood and focus on the fact that I am not alone in this. When I am feeling insecure about my failures, I need time to confess to God my inadequacy for this job and to admit my utter dependence on Him. When I am feeling smug about parenting victories, I need time to be reminded that I am nothing without Him. When I am confused, I need time to spend in His presence, listening for His guidance and searching in His Word. When I'm too self-absorbed, I need time to pray for other people's needs. Time spent with God, every day, offers the ultimate getaway, not to indulge the flesh, but to renew the soul.

Every mom has her share of goofs, mistakes, and bad days! But prayer is the underpinning. Prayer is the foundation. Prayer is the key that will unlock the potential these years hold—for you and for your children. Why, then, is the matter of a daily time with God relegated to life's discount rack? Why is it in last place instead of first? And why is it so hard to establish and maintain?

Break Down the Barriers

A lack of discipline is the main hindrance in maintaining a daily quiet time. "I'm very cyclical," shares Amy, a mother of two in Tallahassee, Florida. "I'll do it for a few days, and then I quit making an effort."

Discipline, or self-control, is best illustrated by Olympic athletes. They spend extensive hours in physical training, sacrificing in pursuit of a goal. Their rigorous determination does not take shortcuts or struggle with laziness. What is their secret? Desire. They are motivated by how desperately they want the gold medal.

I have struggled so much throughout my life with the double-edged sword of perfectionism and procrastination, especially when it comes to managing my home. I was actually writing an article on organization for *ParentLife*, and I called Kathy Peel's office the day before my article was due to ask for an interview. While I was convinced this was something Kathy Peel, known as America's Family Manager and author of *Desperate Households*, would never have to do, I swallowed my pride and did it anyway.

The secretary answered and told me Kathy was on vacation. She gave me her personal e-mail and told me that would be the best way to get in touch with her. So I decided to go for it. I wrote Kathy and explained my situation. Within a couple of hours, she called me. What a lovely, gracious woman! She told me something that I have never forgotten. You see, I thought you had to be born organized in order to have a clean, well-maintained home. I had wrongly assumed that Kathy was just born organized and that it all came naturally to her. But she shared with me that she was organizationally challenged as a young mom. She was motivated to make changes when she finally realized her personal weakness in the area of organization was bringing a great deal of stress on her family. How, then, did she have the discipline to make a lifestyle change that put new strategies in place? "It's a matter of how desperate you are to create a home that is peaceful for raising the kids," she said.[53] I soon began to realize that desperation motivates the desire that expresses itself in discipline.

Now, let's apply that to spiritual matters. How desperate are you to establish an intimate relationship with God? Most Christians are caught in the Apostle Paul's paradox of not doing what they should, but doing what they should not. Jesus said, "The spirit is willing, but the flesh is weak" (Matthew 26:41, NIV). The spirit makes to-do lists, but the flesh does not get them done. The spirit wants to make a grocery list and use coupons, but the flesh goes to the store hungry and buys everything that looks good. The spirit desires a deeper walk with God, but the flesh lets other things crowd in.

Most parents lay enough guilt on themselves without being told they do not pray enough. *Where do I find a balance? What else can I do? What am I doing wrong?*

In the struggle of spirit over flesh, you must come to a place of deeper surrender. Surrender is not about trying harder, it is realizing that God is in control. You have to let go of your preoccupation with yourself. You have to lay down your tendency to take charge, to usurp the authority you relinquished the day you made Christ your Lord. In doing so, you will receive more of God's grace in every area of life, especially when it comes to raising your children. You will be on your way to becoming the parent and the person He wants you to be.

Another barrier to time with God is the simple fact that time itself is in short supply. While it may seem crazy to ask parents to give up any of their already-limited time, it seems even more foolish to expect anyone to function sanely in parenting without quality quiet time every day. Do you need more hours in the day, or do you simply need to rethink your priorities?

Kathy Peel believes, "Time is a resource that God gives us. Every day is a gift." She recommends using a kitchen timer or wristwatch alarm to curtail activities such as long-winded phone calls or nonstop activities that drain your time. "I can't afford to get stuck doing things that are not a part of my daily priorities," she says, and the top priority is her quiet time. "It's important for me to give God the firstfruits of my day," she shares.

A few years ago, I took a very unofficial, unscientific poll of about one hundred women in Florida. I was speaking at a women's conference in Tallahassee, and I handed out a form asking the women to tell me the number one reason why they couldn't have a daily quiet time. Nearly seventy percent of those women said they were too tired—too tired to get up in the morning, too tired to stay up at night.

Fern Nichols, founder and president of Moms In Touch International and mother of four, knows about being tired. "The biggest number that Satan wants to pull on a young mom is her guilt over not spending time with the One she says she loves—her Heavenly Father," Fern says.[54] She insists, however, that something is better than nothing when it comes to a quiet time.

"There's something about the stillness and the quietness of the heart, even for just a few moments, that can help a mom really remember who she is," she explains. Fern advises moms to praise God, even if they have just a few minutes of time. Two or three moments dwelling on God's Lordship, supremacy, or wisdom will help a mom throughout the day. "She's going to realize that God is in control," says Fern. "There's nothing about her day that God is not going to help her with."

Work a Plan

Create a hideaway. Do you have a safe place where you can retreat every day? Moms want to be available to their young children at all times, but there needs to be a place where you can shut out the world and focus on God. One mom I know put a pillow and lap desk on the floor of her closet. She sneaks there in the mornings to pray and journal her thoughts. Susannah Wesley, the eighteenth century mother of John and Samuel Wesley (and seventeen others), found her sanctuary by throwing her apron over her head so that it covered her face. This was her escape; her brood understood she was talking to God and could not be interrupted.

Of course, your living room, bedroom, or kitchen table will work great as a place of retreat, too. Just keep in mind that a daily retreat offers time for clear thinking only when distractions are eliminated.

Collect your resources. Where are your Bible study

materials? If you have left them in the car, you are not going to want to go outside and get them on a cold, wintry morning. My friend Cathy keeps a basket beside her bed. It holds her Bible, journal, and study books, along with a stash of note cards, envelopes, and stamps. Cathy says that when God prompts her to pray for someone, He often urges her to send that person an encouraging note or a verse of Scripture as well. She is prepared to be a channel of God's love when she has her daily retreat.

Another option is to keep your things in a tote bag so you can grab it and take it along to a child's music lesson or sports practice. Spending thirty minutes studying while you wait in a quiet car is the perfect time to retreat with the Lord. Many times a mom's hectic schedule does not allow for a regularly scheduled block of time to retreat every day. In that case, having your resources on hand makes it convenient to take advantage of any quiet moment that comes your way.

Connect with an accountability partner. It is important to connect with a friend who will help you keep this daily date with God. Amy, a mother of two, shared with an older woman in her church that she longed for time with God, but with her busy schedule she didn't see how it could be done. "I'll pray for you," the lady said, "and I'll call you." The very next night, the woman called Amy at nine o'clock.

"Have you had time with the Lord today?" she asked.

"No, I'm afraid not," Amy replied. "I just got the kids in bed."

"Why don't you go do it now?" the lady suggested. Amy's mentor called every night until Amy had established her evening retreat. The calls tapered to once a week, then once a month. Amy credits her accountability partner with having enough concern and love for her to help her establish a closer walk with Christ.

Consider your example. While a retreat is a time to pull away from others and focus on God, consider your children's interruptions an opportunity to teach them the importance of spending time with God every day. When my children were very young, they often "caught" me having prayer and Bible study. When this happened, I would allow them to join me in prayer or listen as I read my Scripture and devotion aloud to them. I always emphasized to them, however, my need to be alone with God and asked them to respect my morning time. As they have gotten older, I have been blessed to see them reading the Bible as they start or end the day. Initially, I asked them to have a quiet time each day, and to help establish it as a habit, we adhered to a phrase I picked up from author Elisabeth Elliot: "No Bible, no breakfast." Helping their children establish that daily morning quiet time was so important to Mrs. Elliot's parents that she and her siblings knew they had to feed themselves spiritually before they would be served breakfast. Some might question this method or think it to be legalistic; however, I have found that without a habit firmly in place, the day moves on rather quickly, and the time that could have been spent with the Lord is forever lost.

Michelle Duggar told me about a dark time in her life, a time when connecting with God seemed almost impossible. I share her story below, confident that many of us moms can relate.

In the beginning, I really believed I could do it all! I

believed I was capable. But then I journeyed through a season in my life when I had to realize that it was not about me. I am not Supermom, and I never will be. I had to give my expectations to God and realize that it was Him working through me.

I was carrying Joseph, my seventh, and I went through a time of great spiritual warfare. When you are in the middle of it, you do not realize what is going on. I just remember how I struggled with reading my Bible, and I cried, and I asked Jim Bob to pray for me. It seemed as though there was a dark heaviness hanging over my personal devotions and my time alone with the Lord.

The Lord reminded me of something I once heard a pastor say. His message was that our quiet times are vital. He said at times, it will be like eating peaches and cream. At other times, it will be like taking your vitamins. You know you need to do it, and so you do. I realized that for me, it was a time in my life that everything seemed overwhelming, and I was struggling so, and I prayed, "Lord, I've got to fill my mind with Your Word because You're the one with all the answers. You've got all the truth and all knowledge, and I need help! I just can't do it for myself. I can't even seem to bring the spoon to my mouth. It's like I'm paralyzed."

The thought occurred to me that I must feed myself intravenously with the Word of God. So I began to listen to the Bible on tape. I listened throughout the day and night. I popped in a tape while I worked in the kitchen. While I was preparing meals and feeding the children, I listened to God's Word.

I had never struggled with insomnia or fears at any other time in my life, until this time of spiritual warfare. For the first time, I had bad dreams, fears, and insomnia. I put a Bible tape on continuous play so that when I could not sleep, I could listen to God's Word. It ministered to my heart in an amazing way. It was so empowering! It was as though God was letting me know that I could never saturate myself too much with His Truth and His Word.

It is not in my strength that I am parenting these children. It is not my organizational skills or my administrative abilities. It is not my loving kindness! I had to come to the place of admitting that I am not capable, but I will glory in my infirmities that the power of Christ may rest upon me. That is what I want my children to see when they look in my face: not "Momma," but Jesus, coming through me to them. I want them to know Him. I want each of them to have a personal relationship with Him, and I want them to walk with Him. [55]

Daily Bible study and prayer, whether you get to have a good long time to feast in the Word or if you just get a snack, are imperative for successful living. When your spiritual disciplines are in place, your faith is stable, your heart is wise, and your spirit is in tune with the Father's. Abide in Him.

Toolbox ────────────────

GETTING STARTED

Get to bed on time. Your quiet time starts the night before. Plan for it.

Start with fifteen minutes. Set the alarm. Ask God to help you get up.

Read the Proverbs. Proverbs is divided into thirty-one chapters, one for each day of the month. Perfect!

Talk to God. Many people use the acronym ACTS for guiding their prayers.

A Adoration. Praise God by listening to a worship song, singing, or just speaking aloud of His many praiseworthy attributes.

C Confession. If something is troubling you, an old habit, a misspoken word, a selfish deed, confess it to the Lord and ask for forgiveness.

T Thanksgiving. Thank Him for everything, one at a time! Further cultivate a thankful heart by keeping a thankfulness journal. Jotting down a few things you are thankful for each night is a great way to end the day.

S Supplication. Once you've completed the first three steps, your mind is clear and your heart is ready to make your true requests known to God.

ELEVEN

THE INSUFFICIENCY OF
AN IMMATURE FAITH

Several years ago, God called my husband to do something so strange that there wasn't even a name for it. Rich felt led to leave our midsized suburban church, where together, we led a thriving Sunday school class of young married couples and, for lack of a better term, venture out to "Sunday school plant." He believed God was calling him, and consequently, our family, to step out of our nice, comfortable church and go to a church where we would be more needed. God began directing Rich specifically and deliberately. The Lord's call was so clear, in fact, that when Rich went to the pastor of the church where God had led him, he said, "I believe God wants me to come here and help you with your Sunday school program." And the pastor, wide-eyed, pulled a card from his pocket on which he had written his prayer requests. At the top of the list, he had scrawled, "I need help with Sunday school." So, after guiding us out of our suburban, progressive, who-could-ask-for-anything-more church, God's footprints stopped at the doors of an inner city, dated, we-need-everything church. Our kids were eleven, nine, and six at the time.

I began the journey patting myself on the back for being a submissive wife. "If the Lord is leading Rich, then He's leading all of us," I told my friends cheerfully. However, after a couple of weeks, I'm quite ashamed to admit there wasn't a submissive bone in my body. I simply didn't want to be there.

Following Rich meant our children had been asked to leave a church full of kids, friends they had grown up with, to go to a much smaller church and start over with a few kids they did not know. Truthfully, I found my kids confronting life issues in the city that I did not have to worry about in the suburbs. I was unsure about this new environment. Most of the children who did attend were dropped off and picked up by parents who never even came in the building. We were on the world's front lines, and it was a far cry from my happy, safe church. I questioned God and wrestled with what He was doing in my husband's life. One Sunday after we arrived home from church, I told Rich, "Look, I believe you're called, but I sure don't know what I'm doing there. I'm lonely. There's no one there like me." I have no doubt it was the voice of God speaking through my husband as he gently replied, "Maybe we're not supposed to go to church to be with people who are like us."

Safe Kids or Strong Kids?

Dr. Tim Kimmel is a speaker, family advocate, and author of several books, including *Why Christian Kids Rebel*.[56] The day

I had the privilege of chatting with him, one of the things we talked about was the subject of raising safe kids as opposed to strong kids. I had never thought about it in those terms before. Dr. Kimmel said, "Most parents are preoccupied with raising safe kids. That is not our job. Our job is to raise strong kids, not safe ones. The reason they want to raise safe ones is that it's easier for them as a parent. But my job is to send my kids on into the future able to stand on their own two feet by God's power."

Did I believe the object of the game was to raise safe kids? Yes, I would have classified myself as one of those parents, especially at the beginning. My tendency was to shield my kids from anything even remotely harmful. We live in a land of bus stop abductions and sexual predators, substance abuse and drug addictions, rampant childhood diseases, and the constant threat of terrorists, the bird flu, and tainted tacos. It is a scary time and place to be raising a child! But even then, during the early years of parenting, a phrase from a book I read was tagged on the walls of my mind. Donna Otto, in her book, *The Stay-at-Home Mom*, wrote about mothering in order to present little saints to the King.[57] That is a beautiful, romanticized picture until you really let it sink in. The road to sainthood isn't safe; in fact, one of the surest ways to get there is to be martyred. That isn't safe at all.

Dr. Kimmel said, "Parents make the mistake of protecting their kids all the way. They don't bring them up to speed, because to bring them up to speed means you must put them at risk. I'm not saying throw them to the wolves. I'm saying there's a way that you gradually introduce the challenges that their culture surrounds them with and then show them: This is how we stand for God in the middle of this. This is how we appropriate the power of the Holy Spirit. This is how we apply the Bible, and this is what we do when we fail, when we fall short: We reconcile with God." We begin by protecting, but gradually, we must move to preparing our children to make their own wise decisions, choosing to follow Christ in every aspect of their lives.

Remember child-proofing your home? Rich and I put child locks on the kitchen cabinets. We bought a playpen and a baby gate. We installed plastic covers on all the electrical outlets. Today, however, my home is far from child-proofed. When my young nephew and nieces come over, I'm nearly thrown into a panic! I don't feel ready because we let our guards down a long time ago. The cabinets are no longer on lock-down because our kids know how to use cleaners properly. They've learned how to get safely up and down stairs. They can even stay home alone. And everyone at my house is familiar with electrical outlets and what not to stick in them. The goal was not to protect them forever. The goal was to prepare them. It works the same way spiritually. As your guard goes down, your child's guard, the Holy Spirit working in his heart, is going up. Your home is a training ground for teaching your children how to react to a lost world and the tempting choices it offers by making the Bible applicable, the Holy Spirit noticeable, and God's forgiveness accessible.

My sons and I were watching a rerun of *The Cosby Show* one evening when the trailer for an R-rated movie came on. I could not find the remote fast enough, and my boys were exposed to something obscene and immoral before I could do anything about it. I was angry because the ad came on during a show I thought of as "safe." Dr. Kimmel would challenge me to use the opportunity as a lesson on how we apply Christ's teachings to our lost world. "When you are really walking closely and intimately with the Holy Spirit, you get troubled by the things you see, not offended," he explains. A lost world cannot be expected to act Christlike or to be entertained by wholesomeness. By simply explaining that Jesus came to save sinners, and even stopping to pray, I could have shared more of Christ's character with my children that night. "We are not given biblical freedom to stand in condemnation of lost people," shares Dr. Kimmel. "In fact, the most famous verse in the Bible is John 3:16, but its punch line is John 3:17. It says, 'For God did not send His Son into the world to condemn the world, but that the world through Him might be saved.'"

My friend Jan's son Daren[58] had been invited to friend's birthday party. One of the planned activities was a movie Daren knew he was not allowed to watch. He occupied himself with Legos in another part of the house and rejoined the group when the movie was over. The parents of the birthday boy called Jan to rave about what a great kid she had! They found it incredible that an eleven-year-old boy would be obedient to parents who would never know if he chose to go against their wishes. Jan recalls, "I had been hesitant to let him go to this party. I knew the other boy's parents were not exactly on the same wavelength with me on a number of issues. But I trusted Daren because I trusted God working in him." According to Dr. Kimmel, Jan did the right thing. "We should not let our fears dictate our plan of parenting," he explains. "We should let our confidence in the power of God set the stage for how we do what we do." By overprotecting our middlers, we miss opportunities for them to exercise what Dr. Kimmel describes as the very system God designed to protect them: the presence of the Holy Spirit in their hearts.

When my daughter was eleven, she was spending the night at a friend's house while I was speaking at a weekend conference. She had been wanting to see a certain movie that had just come out on video, but our family policy then was that we watched movies together (remote in hand) or after my husband and I had previewed it. We had not had time to do either one. Danya called to tell me her friend had the movie.

"Mom," she said, "Ashton has the movie I've wanted to see. Do you care if I watch it?"

"Honey," I said, "I do care. You girls do something else, and we'll talk about the movie after the conference."

"Yes, ma'am," she said.

As soon as I hung up the phone, God began nudging my heart. I reflected on the conversation with my daughter. Danya could have said a number of things in response. She could have said, "But Miss Vicki is one of your best friends, and she thinks the movie is all right." Or she could have said, "Ashton is two years younger than me, and she's already seen it!" I could only imagine the arguing and cajoling I would have probably pulled had I been in her shoes. It struck me then that my daughter had shown a great deal of maturity, first in calling, then in accepting my answer. She was growing up, and I needed to let her know that I noticed. I needed to applaud the character God was building in her. So I called her back.

"Danya," I said, "you honored me just now. As soon as we get home, you and I will rent that movie and have a girls' night. You honored me, and now I want to honor you."

We got home and hit the video store the very next day. The video she wanted was on sale, used, for six dollars. To rent it would have been three dollars, so I did something I never do and went ahead and bought it. That evening was a special mother-daughter time for us. The movie turned out to be really good, initiated a lot of conversations, and it remains one of our favorites. I realized then it was time for me to loosen up and allow her to begin practicing making good viewing choices on her own, not just to please me, but to please God.

That's the goal, isn't it? After all, we're not always going to be there to hold the remote, or the mouse, or the (gasp!) car keys. This is our kids' training ground, now, while they are at home. This is the time to train their hearts.

As a young mom, I was always so sincerely stunned when my children got in trouble. For some reason, I expected them to be perfect. I often took it quite personally when they were disobedient, and I shouldn't have. Of course, I got over it, and I also got over trying to be a perfect mom. At best, my failures present the opportunity for me to teach my kids the truth of God's grace and forgiveness. It's real. It's available. It's essential because no one is perfect. I cannot expect the middle school years to go by without any difficulties. "Our kids are going to make mistakes," Kimmel states. "That's okay. That's not the end of the world. Jesus is in the redemption business. He's all about hope."

As Christian parents, we pour ourselves into our children.

We literally invest our lives in them, praying for a return on the investment that will yield a great harvest for the Kingdom of God. But often we are lacking when it comes to truly engaging our kids' hearts and steering them toward a God-honoring fidelity (faithfulness). What we are really after is for them to enter into a heart-to-heart relationship with the living, actively present person of Jesus Christ.

James E. Gilman, author of *Fidelity of Heart: An Ethic of Christian Virtue*, believes this depth of relationship with Christ will not happen without apprenticeship.[59] "Without apprenticeship, there is only a generation of youth who admire Jesus but have not been taught how to follow Him," he explains. "Without apprenticeship learning, there is no fidelity of heart because fidelity of heart is learning how to do and how to think, and not just what to say and where to be."

Gilman believes that when it comes to training children, today's Christian parents are successful on many fronts. "We engage our children's minds by teaching them true and correct beliefs. We connect their souls through worship, devotions, and church attendance. We unite their bodies with other believers through socializing and fellowship."

But what we are doing in these instances is teaching our children to admire Jesus, not to actually, behaviorally follow Him. "All of these things are necessary to follow Christ," says Gilman, "but by themselves, they are churning out Christian spectators. It is only by doing that we can claim to be followers and not merely admirers of Jesus."

Fan or Follower?

I am a baseball fan. In fact, my family would tell you that

when it comes to my favorite major league team, I am a fanatic. I wear my lucky team shirt and cap to watch their games on TV, and from my comfy spot on the couch, I yell, scream, fuss, and fume. I know all of the players' names, and I even have my favorites, going so far as to solicit their baseball cards from my sons.

The truth of the matter, however, is that I will never be a baseball player. I will always be a spectator, an admirer of the sport—a fan. I will never step up to the plate and hit a line drive or even a fly ball. I will never run the bases or play left field. The closest I have ever gotten is going to a game and taking pictures during batting practice—the actions of an onlooker, not a participant. It's fun being a fan, but my fanaticism does not transform anyone's life. It does not give anyone hope. It does not bring healing. In short, it does not make a difference.

This is where the adventure of missional living comes in. The term *missional* is actually a combination of two words, *mission* and *intentional*. This is what Christ's ministry was all about. It is purposeful Christianity that seeks to join Christ in the daring rescues of the lost from the very gates of Hell. That's exciting! That's adventure! That's the passion that will rescue our middle schoolers from the threshold of apathy, where attraction to the world begins and nonchalance toward Christ threatens the flame you've spent years fanning.

Missional living calls for a return to apprenticeship. An apprentice is one who learns a skill from a master teacher, and the greater part of the learning takes place on the job. "This was Jesus' principle way of teaching," says Gilman. Jesus took His disciples with Him on His journeys, modeling compassion and love, showing them how to preach, teach, and pray. His daily instruction, confirmed by His own life, showed them holy habits, attitudes, and emotions.

We have a tremendous opportunity to apprentice our children and to provide opportunities for them to learn from others. When I look back on the past several years that we have spent in our inner-city church, I see numerous ways that God has allowed our family to apprentice. Some are:

- Servant ministry—Serving those who can never pay us back.

- Community ministry—Assisting in programs designed to help the people around us with felt needs, such as groceries, budgeting, income tax preparation, and computer education, all designed to engage them in relationships. These relationships then give us the opportunity to point them to their spiritual need for Jesus.

- Children's ministry—Building relationships with children we would have never known and being there to love them through their hurts.

I realize, too, that it was all part of God's plan for our family. My kids are different. They wouldn't be the same kids they are today if we had stayed where everyone was like us. They have been around kids who come from very different backgrounds, but at the same time, they have been around kids who come from a very different spiritual perspective. Their desperate need for God is not camouflaged by the many luxuries of life, not just material goods, but things like a safe home environment and parents who love each other. For many of these kids, church itself is a luxury. It is not something they take for granted. It is a safe place, a refuge. It is where they get hugs and attention, and often, a good meal. It is the only place in their lives where God is honored.

These are kids who don't come to church because it is their habit. They aren't there because someone woke them and told them to get ready. They aren't dressed in their Sunday best with their tummies full from a nourishing breakfast. They come while their parents stay home in bed. They come because they want to be there.

While following my husband's lead in making the move was not easy for any of us, I knew Danya was taking it pretty hard. She was at that age when friends begin to be terribly important, and there were no girls her age at the new church. I remember praying for my daughter and asking God to show her why she was there. Not why *we* were there, but why *she* was there. If God had called her dad, then He had called us all, and He would have a purpose for each of us. Within about six months, Danya moved up to the youth department, where their fledgling teen worship band needed a keyboardist. That was it. That was the slot my girl was made to fill. Weekly band practice gave her new friends; they were all older, but she fit right in. The teens began leading worship for a contemporary service we held on Sunday nights. And within a year, God took those kids and had them on Nashville's famous Music Row cutting a CD of worship songs. Amazing!

Active ministry serving a living Jesus changed my daughter from a mere Jesus fan to a radical Jesus follower. The kids I was at first apprehensive about were the very ones who ended up challenging us all to rise to the risk of our faith. That's what I want for my kids and for me, too. We have seen for ourselves the needy, lost world. And that's a good thing because we have a worthy, able Savior in Christ.

Ah, the middle school years—a season of change! For kids, it means transitioning from child to young adult. For you as a parent, it means actively and intentionally stepping up to the parenting plate everyday, determined to keep your eyes on whatever pitch is thrown. It might be a curveball. It might be a little outside. It might knock you down. Determine to live for Jesus no matter what! This is the passion that will expose—in loving, living color—the mystery of Christ in you! In the bottom of the ninth, the outcome of the game is not up to the fans. It is up to the followers.

Toolbox

APPRENTICE YOUR CHILD

Provide role models. Give them the opportunity to be around mature Christ-followers: grandparents, pastors, teachers, and leaders in your church.

Be real. Share your struggles. Pray together.

Discover internships. An internship provides a chance for your child to get a glimpse of a job or ministry they are interested in. Let them volunteer for an hour a week to work alongside a pastor, a realtor, or a business owner.

Lead them to serve. Think food pantries, clothes closets, and soup kitchens.

Lead them to encourage. They can learn how to write encouraging letters to missionaries or homebound members of your church. How about visiting a local children's hospital with a fun book to read to the patients?

Work with them. Together, adopt a stretch of highway to keep clean or rake an elderly neighbor's leaves (free of charge, of course!).

Share your passion. What is your passion? What did you love doing for Jesus before you had kids? They are old enough now to do it with you.

ABOUT THE AUTHOR

Rebecca Ingram Powell is the author of *Baby Boot Camp: Basic Training for the First Six Weeks of Motherhood* (for new and expectant moms), *Wise Up! Experience the Power of Proverbs*, *Get Real! Embrace the Reality of Ruth* (for teen girls), and *Dig Deep: Unearthing the Treasures of Solomon's Proverbs* (for teen guys). Since 2002, Rebecca has been a monthly columnist for *ParentLife* magazine (LifeWay Christian Resources), writing the popular feature "Mom's Life."

As a speaker, Rebecca ministers at women's events, girls' conferences, parenting seminars, and homeschool conventions, often with teen daughter, Danya, serving as worship leader. Sharing personal stories from her life today and candidly connecting through her memories of life as a teen, Rebecca reaches the hearts of her listeners. Her dynamic speaking style is real and warm, loaded with humor, and grounded in biblical truth.

Rebecca and her husband, Rich, have been married for twenty years and today live in a suburb of Nashville, Tennessee, with their three children, Danya, David, and Derek. The

Powells are members of First Baptist Church, Madison, where Rich serves bi-vocationally as Minister of Missions.

To contact Rebecca, learn more about her resources, view her speaking topics, or schedule a conference event, please visit www.rebeccapowell.com.

ENDNOTES

Chapter One

1 Quotes taken from personal interview conducted with Brandon James for *ParentLife* magazine.

2 Name has been changed.

Chapter Two

3 Wallis, Claudia. "Is Middle School Bad for Kids?" *Time* 01 Aug 05. <http://www.time.com/time/magazine/article/0,9171,1088694,00.html>

4 "The Bermuda Triangle." 05 December 2007 <http://byerly.org/bt.htm>

5 Quotes taken from personal interview conducted with Joyce Pelletier for *ParentLife* magazine.

Chapter Three

6 Gibbs, Nancy. "Being 13." *Time* 31 July 2005. <http://

www.time.com/time/magazine/article/0,9171,1088701–3,00.html>

7   "Andre Agassi." *Wikipedia, The Free Encyclopedia.* 28 May 2007, 13:43 UTC. Wikimedia Foundation, Inc. 2 Jun 2007 <http://en.wikipedia.org/w/index. php?title=Andre_Agassi&oldid=134073963>

8   Smith, Gary. "Steroids and Baseball: What Do We Do Now?" *Sports Illustrated* 28 Mar 2005: 40–50.

9   Zickler, Patrick. "NIDA Initiative Targets Increasing Teen Use of Anabolic Steroids." NIDA Notes. <http://www. nida.nih.gov/NIDA_notes/NNv0115N3/Initiative. html> 060207

10   Powell, Rebecca Ingram. *Dig Deep: Unearthing the Treasures of Solomon's Proverbs.* Enumclaw: Pleasant Word, 2006.

11   Woodruff, Paul. *Reverence: Renewing a Forgotten Virtue.* New York: Oxford University Press, 2001.

12   Tripp, Paul David. *Age of Opportunity: A Biblical Guide to Parenting Teens.* Phillipsburg: P & R Publishing, 2001.

Chapter Four

13   Omartian, Stormie. *The Power of a Praying Parent.* Eugene: Harvest House, 1997.

14   See Colossians 4:12.

15   Thayer and Smith. "Greek Lexicon entry for Agonizomai." *The KJV New Testament Greek Lexicon.* <http://www.biblestudytools.net/Lexicons/Greek/grk. cgi?number=75&version=kjv>

16   See Matthew 6.

17   See Colossians 4:12.

18 Name has been changed.

19 Powell, Rebecca Ingram. Illustration adapted from *Wise Up! Experience the Power of Proverbs*. Enumclaw: Pleasant Word, 2005.

20 See 1 Peter 5:8.

21 See Proverbs 3:7.

22 See Judges 13:3–14.

23 Plowman, Ginger. *Don't Make Me Count to Three!* Wapwallopen: Shepherd Press, 2003.

Chapter Five

24 Califano, Joseph A. "A Weapon in the War on Drugs: Dining In." Virginia Education Association. <http://www.veaweteach.org/resources_parents_detail.asp?ContentID=413>

25 Quotes taken from personal interview conducted with Leanne Ely for *ParentLife* magazine.

26 Quotes taken from personal interview conducted with Tom and Jeannie Elliff for *HomeLife* magazine.

27 Quotes taken from personal interview conducted with Michelle Duggar for *ParentLife* magazine.

28 Chismar, Janet. "Dennis Rainey Says, 'Give Them the Gift of You at Christmas.'" <http://www.crosswalk.com/faith/1302506.html>

Chapter Six

29 Name has been changed.

30 Hempel, Jessi. "The MySpace Generation." *Business*

Week. 12 December 2005. <http://www.businessweek. com/magazine/content/05_50/b3963001.htm>

31 See 2 Corinthians 6:14.

32 Omartian, Stormie. *The Power of a Praying Parent*. Eugene: Harvest House, 1997.

33 Kimmel, Dr. Tim. *Why Christian Kids Rebel: Trading Heartache for Hope*. Nashville: W Publishing Group, 2004.

34 See James 5:16.

35 Name has been changed.

36 Powell, Rebecca Ingram. Story adapted from *Dig Deep: Unearthing the Treasures of Solomon's Proverbs*. Enumclaw: Pleasant Word, 2006.

Chapter Seven

37 Quotes taken from personal interview conducted with Clay Crosse for *ParentLife* magazine.

38 Name has been changed.

39 Quotes taken from personal interview conducted with Jay Younts for *ParentLife* magazine.

40 Rebecca recommends mothers and daughters listen together to her audio message, "The Modesty CD," available at www.rebeccapowell.com.

Chapter Eight

41 Harris, Joshua. *I Kissed Dating Goodbye*. Colorado Springs: Multnomah, 1997.

42 Powell, Rebecca Ingram. *Get Real! Embrace the Reality of Ruth*. Enumclaw: Pleasant Word, 2007.

43 Name has been changed.

44 McDowell, Josh and Dick Day. *Why Wait?* San Bernardino: Here's Life Publishers, 1987.

45 See Genesis 2:21–22.

46 See Genesis 24.

47 Wu, Janet. "Cancer Cure." Air date: 8 Nov 2002. http://www1.whdh.com/features/articles/healthcast/H1153/

Chapter Nine

48 Quotes taken from personal interview conducted with Robert Lewis for *ParentLife* magazine.

49 Quotes taken from personal interview conducted with Timm Glover for *ParentLife* magazine.

50 Powell, Rebecca Ingram. "Beyond the Lemonade Stand." *ParentLife* May 08.

51 Quotes taken from personal interview conducted with Patricia Sprinkle for *ParentLife* magazine.

52 See 2 Timothy 3:16.

Chapter Ten

53 Quotes taken from personal interview conducted with Kathy Peel for *ParentLife* magazine.

54 Quotes taken from personal interview conducted with Fern Nichols for Pastors.com.

55 Quotes taken from personal interview conducted with Michelle Duggar for *ParentLife* magazine.

Chapter Eleven

56 Quotes taken from personal interview conducted with Dr. Tim Kimmel for *ParentLife* magazine.

57 Otto, Donna. *The Stay-at-Home Mom: For Women at Home and Those Who Want to Be.* Eugene: Harvest House, 1997.

58 Names have been changed.

59 Quotes taken from personal interview conducted with James E. Gilman for *ParentLife* magazine.